A
Security
Professional's
Practical Guide to the Law

David L. Ray, B.A., LL.B.

Aurora Professional Press
a division of Canada Law Book Inc.
240 Edward St., Aurora, Ontario, L4G 3S9
www.canadalawbook.ca

The paper used in this publication meets the minimum requirements of American National Standards for Information Sciences — Permanence of Paper for Printed Library Materials ANSI Z39.48-1992.

National Library of Canada Cataloguing in Publication

Ray, David L. (David Lawrence), 1944-
  A security professional's practical guide to the law / David L. Ray.

Includes index.
ISBN 0-88804-401-1

  1. Private security services—Canada. 2. Police, Private—Legal status, laws, etc.—Canada. I. Title.

KE450.P65R39 2004   344'.7105289   C2004-902195-8
KF390.P65R39 2004

Foreword

If you are a working security professional or training to be one, you need to know what powers of enforcement are available to you as well as what protections are afforded to those who might be accused of misconduct and criminal activity. The impact of privacy legislation on your work, the distinctions between civil and criminal acts, a clear understanding of employee and employer rights and obligations in both union and non-union environments and the definitions of property and Charter rights, all are matters of vital interest and importance to you. Before you engage in providing security services to a client, you need to understand the legal requirements that will be demanded of you with respect to surveillance activities, if undertaken, and in the event of legal proceedings, the gathering, presentation and admissibility of evidence. In addition to providing you with this essential information, *A Security Professional's Practical Guide to the Law* promotes the development of the critical thinking skills you will require if you are to perform appropriately and adequately under Canadian law.

This book is a response to the urgent need to provide security professionals with basic information about the legal aspects of their work. The author, a practising security professional and former police officer and lawyer, has the first-hand knowledge and practical experience that afford readers the benefit of a considered and comprehensive perspective on private security law.

April, 2004

Glen Kitteringham, M.Sc., CPP
Senior Manager Security and Life Safety
Brookfield Properties

Preface

It is my hope that security professionals who read this book will come to understand that they do not work in isolation. From the security officer on patrol reporting suspicious activity to an employer, to the trained emergency response team reacting to a threat of imminent danger to the public peace, security work is performed within the same legal context. It is that context that all security professionals need to understand in order to serve and protect.

Through the use of case studies, analysis and the examination of fundamental Canadian legal tenets, readers will discover key concepts critical to the effective performance of private security work. My goal is to provide a plain language description of how our legal system has evolved and instruction on how to identify, evaluate and manage the legal issues that particularly impact those engaged in this industry.

I wish to acknowledge the fundamental role that participation in professional associations, such as the Canadian Society for Industrial Security and the American Society for Industrial Security, and collaboration with other security professionals and colleagues have contributed to the development of this book. The increased complexity and technological sophistication of surveillance tools and techniques in present day society demand that, with respect to their use, security professionals exhibit an equally rigorous understanding of individual and societal rights and obligations. The purpose of this book, therefore, is to provide a roadmap of basic legal information for security professionals as they navigate the issues that confront them in their daily practice. It is not intended in any way to replace legal counsel. Rather, the information offered in these pages is designed to lead security professionals to consider the legal ramifications of their role and ask the pertinent questions that need to be asked in order to perform their role with confidence and knowledge.

Without the encouragement and patience of my wife, Barbara, and the able editorial assistance of Lynn Machan-Gorham, this book would not have been possible. Their suggestions, contributions and meticulous attention to detail are gratefully acknowledged.

Calgary, Alberta   David Ray
April, 2004

Table of Contents

2 Human Rights 27

3 The Canadian Charter of Rights and Freedoms 45

4 Privacy Legislation and the Duties of Security to Protect Privacy 53

5 Criminal Law 65

7 Security and Human Resource Law 115

8 Evidence 131

Introduction

A security officer goes on rounds.
A dog handler guides his dog through a warehouse sniffing for illegal drugs.
Armed guards exit a bank, bags in hand and board an armoured transport vehicle.
A facilities employee of a corporation begins the process of property identification.
An investigator engages in an inquiry on industrial espionage.
A polygraph test records responses to the statements and questions of an interviewer.
A motion sensor tracks an intrusion and a video camera begins to record it.
A security manager reviews the counter-terrorism procedures of a company.

What these actions have in common is that each of them is undertaken by one or more "agents", acting as contract workers or as staff members of an enterprise, to ensure the private security of that enterprise's people, property, information and reputation. In modern society, there is increasing clear evidence of security professionals at work. In fact, companies that fail to take precautions to protect their physical and intellectual property, their systems and their workers leave themselves vulnerable to serious risk and liability.

What may not be so obvious in each of the above scenarios are the operating principles that apply under Canadian law to ensure that such actions are legally performed. What jurisdiction do private security officers have? How do rights of access, property, information and individual freedoms come into play? We begin by examining the Canadian legal system itself and the concepts of law that govern it. Further on during our examination of private security law, case law will be used to illustrate specific concepts.

1

Private Security Practice and the Canadian Legal System

INTRODUCTION

Many attempts have been made to explain the word "law", but no universally accepted definition exists. To complicate matters, the words "law" and "laws" are applied to a wide variety of precepts, from specific statutes (*e.g.*, the *Criminal Code*) to a whole system of justice (*e.g.*, the Laws of England), as well as to areas outside the justice system (*e.g.*, the law of gravity). The term "law" is also used to describe those who work within our justice system (*e.g.*, law clerk, lawyer and officer of the law). Invariably, each attempt to define the term ends in a circuitous philosophical discussion. For the purposes of this book, therefore, we will define "law" in its broadest sense and examine the Canadian legal system, the lawmakers and the law itself within the context of our society. In simple terms, laws are rules governing society.

Laws are everyday guidelines established by us, by our predecessors and by the governments we elect to make rules. They regulate everyday behaviour, from commerce and leisure to even our most intimate family relationships. The function of our legal system is to stipulate what our obligations are to each other, to set penalties for breaching those obligations and to establish procedures for enforcing their performance.

Considering the broad expectations we have of our legal system, it is small wonder that the law is complex, and it is understandable that even those who have devoted their lives to its study disagree on its meaning and application. The layperson very often holds an overly naive view: are not laws simply statutes that are published in black and white for all to read? A legal practitioner knows otherwise: statutes form only a small part of the entire body of the law.

This chapter is intended to provide the reader with a basic knowledge and understanding of Canadian law and the Canadian legal system. It will examine the various components of the system as well as their origins and evolution.

THE ORIGINS OF THE LAWS WE ENFORCE

There are three significant sources for our present legal system: English common and case law, the French Civil Code and statute law. By reviewing the historical development of these elements, we will better understand our legal system.

Evolution of English and Canadian Common and Case Law

If statutes are the bricks with which the wall is built, the common law is the mortar that holds the bricks together.

During the Dark and Middle Ages in England, the authority to resolve disputes was bestowed upon tribal chieftains or, centuries later, assumed by feudal lords. The power to enforce their decisions resided in the respect in which they were held by those around them (and sometimes in fear of reprisal). The lords were often reluctant to make decisions in many of the more important cases coming before them and, therefore, they resorted to a reliance on divine intervention. Trial by combat and trial by ordeal became commonplace and many strange procedures were developed to settle contentious matters. Perhaps the world's first lie detection system was the requirement that a witness take a mouthful of dry bread and cheese while giving evidence. Choking would then be an indication of a lack of truthfulness. Although these procedures had nothing to do with fairness, justice or truth, as we know it, they certainly removed the burden of judgment from the lord himself.

In spite of this imperfect and rather rough-and-ready form of justice, the populace tended to rely on the fact that the noble would be consistent in his decisions from one trial to the next and would base them on local custom. For this reason it was believed that the application of laws was *common* throughout the land. In fact, this belief was far from reality. It was not until much later in England that a doctrine of precedents developed that would ensure a more universal application of laws.

During the same period on continental Europe, Roman law had established itself as a standard and even after the fall of the Roman Empire its legal principles continued to be entrenched in society. Roman law differed from English common law in that it had been codified by the Emperor Justinian in A.D. 533, whereas English law consisting of verbal decisions and particular customs of the landowners and nobles who adjudicated cases remained unwritten. The Code of Justinian contains a great many similarities to our present-day legal system, including differentiation between public and private law and the importance of equality of the individual. During the feudal age, Roman law declined in importance on the continent. By the 11th century, however, feudal law could no longer meet the more complex legal demands of international trade so that the Justinian Code was again looked upon favourably by scholars and kings.

Consequently, when the Norman king William the Conqueror assumed the throne in England in 1066, he was confronted by a system of courts that based decisions on the customs of the people. Because customs varied in the different areas of the country, the law was inconsistently understood and applied. Although reluctant to impose Roman law on the English, William understood the need for the universal application of the existing laws. He and the Norman kings who followed him were wise enough to allow the English to continue their system of local customs. However, they also established a system of royal courts, appointed judges to those courts and introduced statutes (written law) based on Roman law where necessary to clarify the common law. The legal system practised in Canada today derives from the marriage of these two traditions.

The judges who were appointed in Norman times traveled throughout England and upon their return to London met to discuss their decisions. This procedure ensured greater consistency in the application of the law, but at the same time kept alive the common law tradition of precedents. The meeting places for the judges were the Inns of Court, which institutions continue to exist to this day in modern London. Eventually, the decisions of the judges were written down and reported by secretaries, students of law and interested spectators. Thus was born the first system of *case law*.

By the 13th century, the common law courts had become bogged down under the weight of myriad precedents and procedures and, in many instances, were unable to pronounce judgments that were fair. As a result, appeals to the reigning monarch became the norm in order that "equitable judgments" could be reached. Eventually the king found himself overburdened with appeals, at which point he delegated his authority to the Chancellor and Vice-Chancellors. Courts of Equity (or Chancery) were established, which soon matched the size and complexity of the common law courts. Although each tended to hear different types of cases, vicious legal battles often developed between the parties over which court should have jurisdiction. Finally, in the 19th century, the two systems of courts were combined, in England and Canada, so that now all courts are considered courts of equity.

The Common Law Today

Even with the vast number of statutes in Canada today, the common law plays an important role. By way of illustration, section 9(*a*) of the 1953 version of the *Criminal Code* legislated away all offences at common law with the sole exception of contempt of court. The reality was that few people had been charged with common law offences since 1892 because the codification of those offences into statute law had been virtually completed. Most common law offences are now included in sections of the *Criminal Code*.[1]

The codification did not, however, do away with the common law defences or procedures that had developed over the centuries. As section 8(3) of the *Criminal Code* states:

> 8(3) Every rule and principle of the common law that renders any circumstance a justification or excuse for an act or a defence to a charge continues in force and applies in respect of proceedings for an offence under this Act or any other Act of Parliament except in so far as they are altered by or inconsistent with this Act or any other Act of Parliament.

It would have been difficult, if not impossible, to codify defences and many other procedures of the common law. The *Criminal Code* has, however, addressed the common law defences of mental disorder (section 16), compulsion by threats (section 17) and self-defence (sections 34 to 37). Some examples of common law defences, which are not addressed in the *Criminal Code* but are still available to an accused person, are lack of intent (*mens rea*), drunkenness and necessity. Consider in the case study presented below the following use of self-defence:

> *A store security officer follows a shoplifter out of the store and attempts to arrest him. The shoplifter assaults the officer during the course of the arrest. During the struggle the shoplifter disposes of the stolen item. The shoplifter is charged with theft and resisting arrest but, in court, argues that he is not guilty of the theft because there is no evidence and he is not guilty of resisting arrest because he was acting in self-defence.*

One example of a procedure that developed at common law is the right of police to search a person at the time of arrest. That right is not granted to police in the *Criminal Code* but it exists today because of the establishment of that power at common law (subject to certain qualifications stipulated in the *Canadian Charter of Rights and Freedoms*).[2]

Over time, with the development of case law and the routine documentation of judgments, the doctrine of precedent (*stare decisis*) has become refined and firmly entrenched in law. The doctrine is simple — a court must stand by previous decisions.

The application of *stare decisis,* however, is extremely complex and requires that during trial opposing parties engage in arguments over the

---

[1] The current *Criminal Code* is chapter C-46 of the 1985 *Revised Statutes of Canada* (cited: R.S.C. 1985, c. C-46). For an up-to-date amended version of the *Criminal Code* see *Martin's Annual Criminal Code* (Aurora, Ont.: Canada Law Book), which is available in most public libraries.

[2] Part of the *Constitution Act, 1982.*

precedents that support their causes. Ultimately, the judge must weigh the appropriateness of the presentation of such arguments and associated evidence. The considerations that a judge must weigh when evaluating precedents are described below.

Age of the Case

This may be a two-edged sword. Older cases often set a standard that has become a pillar of the legal system. It was such a case in 1935 that established the measure for the burden of proof in criminal matters (beyond a reasonable doubt) and placed the onus on the Crown to prove the accused guilty.[3] However, changing societal conditions and values can also cause older cases to become outdated and invalid. For example, the standards set in sentencing for the offence of possession of marijuana under the *Controlled Drugs and Substances Act*[4] are vastly different today from what they were in the 1960s. Thus, before citing an older case, a lawyer must also "update" it to ensure that a higher court has not subsequently overturned it or that other courts have not ruled it inapplicable.

Jurisdiction of the Court Where the Decision was Made

Were the precedents under consideration decided in the same jurisdiction, in another province, in another commonwealth country, or in a "foreign" country? A judge of an Ontario court is more likely to look at other Ontario decisions before considering decisions made outside the province or in other countries.

Level of the Court Where the Decision was Made

A judge must follow the previous decisions of higher courts within the same jurisdiction and all courts in Canada are bound by the judgments of the Supreme Court of Canada. This applies, of course, only if the facts in the case being cited are the same as in the case at bar. A judge may also be persuaded by a judgment of a higher court in another province. For several years the common law defence of drunkenness was accepted in the Province of Ontario for the crime of rape (if drunkenness could be proved). The Court of Appeal in British Columbia, however, reached the exact opposite conclusion. As a result, defence counsel in British Columbia could not expect to argue that the client was too drunk to form the intent to commit rape, while in Ontario defence counsel was free to raise that argument. The issue was finally settled in 1977 when the

---

[3] *Woolmington v. Director of Public Prosecutions*, [1935] A.C. 462 (H.L.).
[4] S.C. 1996, c. 19.

Supreme Court of Canada accepted the British Columbia approach and held that drunkenness could not be used as a defence in rape cases.[5]

Similarity of Facts

The cases need not have exactly the same set of facts, but there must be a close resemblance between the facts as they relate to the principle being argued. For example, a theft case in a retail setting reported in case law might be used as precedent in a case before the court for theft of a computer from an office tower because the principles of intent to commit the offence are the same.

Reputation of the Judge Rendering the Decision

Some judges, because of their academic qualifications, years of experience on the bench, or recognized application of fairness and common sense, are particularly respected and their judgments tend to carry more weight.

Whether There Were Any Dissenting Opinions of the Court

Where a decision was unanimous, it will have more weight. But, a well-reasoned dissent may cause the precedent to have less usefulness.

The doctrine of *stare decisis* provides many benefits to our legal system. Lawyers who can find a strong authority (precedent) on point can best determine the likely outcome of a particular cause of action and, therefore, best advise their clients. Precedent also provides the court with a history of previous decisions by other courts and thereby discourages subjective judgments based on whim, especially because there is recourse on appeal to a higher court. Lastly, it provides for consistency in the interpretation of the various statutes.

Civil Law

In order to fully understand the civil law, it is necessary to know the distinction between "public law" and "private law". The terms may vary from country to country, but in Canada the terms may be described as follows.

Public Law

Public laws are those concerned with the relationship between the individual and the state. For example, constitutional law, administrative law, local government and military law, criminal law and criminal procedures fall into this category. They include the laws relied on by security profes-

---

[5]   *R. v. Leary* (1975), 26 C.C.C. (2d) 522, 31 C.R. (N.S.) 199 (B.C.C.A.), affd 33 C.C.C. (2d) 473, [1978] 1 S.C.R. 29.

sionals in protecting property from theft or vandalism and people from assault.

Private Law

Private laws are those concerned with the relationships between individuals. For example, commercial law, family law, torts, property law, trusts, labour law and maritime law fall into this domain. The term "individual" applies to people *and* legal entities. Thus, a contract between the federal government and a corporation may fall within the realm of private law because it is an agreement between two parties even though one of the parties is the state and the other is an entity created by statute. Similarly, a particular act by an individual may fall within both public and private law. For example, security may respond to assist a person who is assaulted by another and may report the matter to the police so that criminal charges can be brought under the *Criminal Code* (public law). At the same time the victim of the assault may sue for battery in order to recover damages (private law).

The French Civil Code

In Canada, the term "civil law" has two separate and distinct meanings: civil law as private law, and civil law as practised in the Province of Quebec and derived from Roman law (*cives Romani*). When discussing the history of Canadian law, we will apply the latter definition.

Even after Canada became a member of the British Empire, civil law remained in effect in Quebec so that today there are nine common law provinces and one civil law province. It is interesting to note that, while common law had a strong influence on criminal law in Quebec, nevertheless, in 1866 the province codified its civil law in accordance with the Code of Napoleon, which had been created in 1804 in France.

In Quebec, a lawyer arguing a case before the criminal courts uses the common law and may rely on precedent of past decisions to interpret a section of the *Criminal Code*. Before a civil court, however, in an action for breach of contract, for example, the same lawyer will rely on the civil code. In the Napoleonic civil code system, large areas of law are covered in very general terms. Although, in Quebec, a judge may rely on previous decisions of other courts, there is greater reliance on the civil code itself and the opinions and legal articles proposed by legal academicians.

To a casual observer of the Quebec civil court system there does not appear to be a vast difference between reliance on the *Civil Code of Quebec*[6] and the Quebec *Code of Civil Procedure*[7] and reliance on the common law in the other nine provinces. Much of the common law in the

---

[6]   S.Q. 1991, c. 64.
[7]   R.S.Q., c. C-25.

latter has been codified (for example, the myriad of consumer protection statutes, sale of goods Acts, etc.) while Quebec relies on precedent for much of its civil law, especially in evidentiary matters. There is a difference in approach, however, and in civil law jurisdictions the codified principles are supreme. By way of example, the police in the civil law jurisdictions of Europe possess only the powers that are granted by law. In Canada, where the *Criminal Code* is based on the common law, the police have any power that is not specifically taken away. Prior to 1973, the police were free to intercept private communications (by wiretapping) because there were no restrictions or laws enacted against such surveillance. With the passage in 1973 of amendments to the *Criminal Code* it became a criminal offence to intercept private communications without a court order.

Statute Law

Prior to 1867, Great Britain enacted all laws governing the colonies that united to become Canada. With the passage of the *British North America Act, 1867* (the "*B.N.A. Act*"),[8] the powers of the British Parliament were transferred to the federal and provincial governments of the new country. The provincial governments, in turn, delegated some of their powers and responsibilities to municipalities within their respective borders. Any legislative authority may also enact statutes that delegate powers and responsibilities to various boards and tribunals. For example, all of the provinces have passed laws that grant authority to the law societies within their jurisdictions to oversee their members. The by-laws passed by these law societies govern everything from qualifications for admission to the bar to disciplinary action for misconduct.

It is possible to raise arguments in court as to whether a legislative authority had the power to enact a particular statute or section of a statute. For instance, if the federal government were to pass a law that fell within one of the heads of section 92 of the *B.N.A. Act*, a lawyer could argue that the legislation was outside the power (*ultra vires*) of Parliament and, therefore, unenforceable.

In summary, Canadian statutes originate from three sources: the Parliament of Canada, provincial legislatures and municipal councils. The respective jurisdictions are spelled out in sections 91 and 92 of the *B.N.A. Act* and are summarized as follows.

---

[8]   This British statute was, in effect, the Constitution of Canada. In 1982 the *British North America Act, 1867* was renamed the *Constitution Act, 1867* at the same time as the Constitution was "repatriated", *i.e.*, declared wholly under the control of the Canadian Government.

91. Federal Jurisdiction

- Public debt and property
- Unemployment insurance
- Borrowing on public credit
- Census and statistics
- Salaries for civil servants
- Navigation and shipping
- Seacoast and inland fisheries
- Currency
- Weights and measures
- Bills of exchange
- Interest
- Bankruptcy
- Copyrights
- Immigration
- Criminal law except the courts
- Everything else not specifically assigned to the provinces
- Trade and commerce
- Taxation
- Postal service
- Defence
- Beacons, buoys, lighthouses and Sable Island
- Quarantine and marine hospitals
- Ferries between provinces or foreign country
- Banking
- Legal tender
- Patents
- Indians and reserves
- Marriage and divorce
- Penitentiaries

92. Provincial Jurisdiction

- Provincial constitutional amendments
- Borrowing on credit of province
- Public lands belonging to province
- Hospitals and charities (except marine hospitals)
- Shop, tavern, auctioneer, other licences
- Incorporation of provincial companies
- Property and civil rights within province
- Non-renewable natural resources, forestry resources and electrical energy[9]
- Direct taxation within province
- Tenure of provincial offices
- Reformatory prisons in and for province
- Municipalities within province
- Local works and undertakings
- Solemnization of marriage
- Administration of justice within province
- Matters of local or private nature in province
- Punishments relating to enforcement of provincial laws

---

[9]   Added by section 50 of the *Constitution Act, 1982.*

Federal Statutes

Federal statutes are laws that are applicable to all of Canada and all Canadians. They may be enacted by Parliament to ensure that there is sufficient revenue to run the country (*e.g.,* customs, excise, income tax), or they may be passed for the protection of the public good (*e.g.,* the *Criminal Code*, weights and measures, fisheries). The *Criminal Code* is a bit unusual in that it is passed and amended by the federal Parliament but administered by the provinces. Note that section 91 of the *B.N.A. Act* assigns authority over "criminal law except the courts" to the federal jurisdiction while section 92 of the Act assigns jurisdiction over the "administration of justice within the province" to the provincial legislatures.

Provincial Statutes

The Legislative Assembly of a province can only pass laws that will apply within the boundaries of that province. The legislature in Saskatchewan cannot pass a law regulating speed limits on the highways in Alberta (and vice versa). Some provincial statutes have federal counterparts (*e.g.,* fisheries, environment) but the jurisdictions of the two statutes differ.

Municipal Statutes

Municipal statutes (also called by-laws or ordinances) are created for peace and good order within the boundaries of the municipality. Municipalities pass laws relating to traffic, garbage removal, zoning, pet control, etc.

How Do Statutes Come into Being?

Like the common law, statutes are constantly being amended, rescinded or replaced. New inventions and discoveries, along with ever-changing world conditions lead to different attitudes and approaches to the way we live. Because of this inevitable evolution of our society, it is necessary to regularly update our statutes to meet new challenges and requirements. As late as the 1930s sections in the *Criminal Code* made it a criminal offence to fail to repel boarders on a vessel. Because the nature of piracy had changed, it was no longer deemed necessary to specify this offence and it was removed from the statute books. Not until the last decade could our legislators have contemplated that air piracy would ever become a problem such that it has been necessary to enact air piracy legislation.

Statutes are created to fill a need in our society. Sometimes those needs are economic (for example, an amendment to the *Income Tax Act* required to "plug a loophole"), and sometimes the need is identified by public opinion (as in changes to the sexual offences sections of the *Criminal Code*). Federal and provincial governments have created law reform commissions to study and monitor various statutes and regulations and make recommendations for amendments.

Legislation governing the security industry has moved forward over the years in some provinces by addressing such issues as requiring that security officers meet a specific training standard in order to be licensed and allowed to practise their profession.

THE COURT SYSTEM IN CANADA

Everyone recognizes that there is a hierarchy of courts in Canada, just as in most other countries. Unfortunately, the Canadian structure is complicated by several factors:

1. The jurisdictions of the courts vary according to the seriousness of the matter. In many cases there is overlapping jurisdiction so that it is often possible for a party to choose the court he or she wishes to proceed in.
2. In some provinces there exists a dual court system, one for civil matters and one for criminal matters, while in others some levels of courts have jurisdiction over both.
3. Some courts act as both a trial court and a court of appeal for decisions originating from lower level courts and tribunals.
4. The courts, although administered by the provinces, hear cases concerning a large number of federal matters. To further complicate things, it is the federal government that has jurisdiction to appoint county and superior court judges under the Constitution.
5. The same court level may be known by different names in different provinces. For example, the Supreme Court of one province may be called the Court of Queen's Bench or the Superior Court in another. Also, jurisdictions all too often rename their courts. This is especially true of Ontario where the present Ontario Superior Court of Justice was previously known as the Ontario Court (General Division), the Ontario Supreme Court and the Ontario High Court of Justice.

The Provincial Courts

First Level

The first level of courts handles a variety of minor civil and criminal matters. They include Small Claims Court, Provincial Court, Surrogate or Probate Court, Family and Juvenile Court. These "specialized" courts are sometimes attached to the second level of courts (*e.g.*, Small Claims may be part of the Court of Queen's Bench or the Superior Court level). Probate or Surrogate Courts are responsible for matters relating to the estates of deceased persons. Family Courts handle matters of family relations other than divorce. Provincial Criminal Courts hear minor criminal matters or hold preliminary inquiries for more serious matters.

Second Level

These are variously titled: Supreme Court, Trial Division; Superior Court; High Court of Justice; or Court of Queen's Bench. This level has "inherent jurisdiction" over any case except those specifically assigned to a lower court. It hears serious criminal and civil matters (*e.g.*, libel actions on the civil side, murder on the criminal side). The amount claimed in damages usually determines whether a civil action will be heard in Small Claims Court or in a court at this level (that amount is established by provincial legislation). These courts also hear first appeals from the underlying court system and from various administrative boards and tribunals.

Third Level

The highest court level in each province is the Court of Appeal (also called the Supreme Court, Appeal (or Appellate) Division or Supreme Court, Court of Appeal). Ontario is the only province with an intermediate appeal court (the Divisional Court). This level hears appeals from the second level of courts. It is not uncommon for an action to skip a level, *e.g.*, to move directly from a board or tribunal to an appeal court.

The National Courts

Supreme Court of Canada

The Supreme Court of Canada is the court of final appeal in Canada.[10] It hears appeals from federal and provincial courts of appeal in all areas of law: criminal, civil, constitutional and administrative law. Located in Ottawa, it is composed of the Chief Justice of Canada and eight puisne (pronounced "puny") judges appointed by the federal government on a regional basis. The panel hearing an appeal may comprise anywhere from three to nine judges, depending on the importance of the matter being heard. The right to have an appeal heard is not automatic and application for "leave to appeal" must be made. By tradition no reasons are given for either granting or refusing "leave" (permission) to appeal. The Supreme Court of Canada (S.C.C.) may also be asked by the federal government to address matters relating to the interpretation of the Constitution, or the legitimacy of any statute or section of a statute particularly, today, as it relates to rights protected by the *Canadian Charter of Rights and Freedoms*. Such cases are referred to as "references".

---

[10] Until 1949, the Judicial Committee of the British Privy Council (P.C.) was the highest appeal court for Canadian cases.

Federal Courts of Canada

The Federal Court, Trial Division (F.C.T.D.) has jurisdiction over matters involving suits against and on behalf of the federal government and matters relating to certain federal statutes, including copyright, patents, trade-marks, bankruptcy, shipping and navigation, immigration and refugee claims. It hears cases in different major cities throughout the country. The Federal Court of Appeal (F.C.A.) hears appeals from the Trial Division and is located in Ottawa. Of course, the final level of appeal is to the Supreme Court of Canada.

Tax Court of Canada

As the name implies, the Tax Court of Canada provides a forum for companies and individuals to settle disagreements arising under federal tax and revenue legislation (income tax, customs and excise). Appeals are handled by the Federal Court, Trial Division and/or the Federal Court of Appeal and finally the Supreme Court of Canada.

Military Courts

Military courts (or court martial courts) are established under the *National Defence Act*[11] to handle military justice and the code of service discipline for the Canadian Armed Forces.

Boards and Tribunals

Both federal and provincial statutes allow for the creation of various boards and tribunals to resolve issues outside of the court system in the interest of speeding up the settlement of grievances and disputes, and thereby reducing the caseload of the courts. Persons with notable expertise in such fields as refugee claims, human rights, labour contracts, insurance and property taxes, for example, hear the arguments of the claimants and defendants and attempt to render an equitable decision. Any disputant who is unhappy with the decision may seek "judicial review" by a higher authority or court. What may have appeared to be a minor grievance at its outset sometimes turns out to have sufficient merit to reach all the way to the Supreme Court of Canada.

Appeals

An appeal may be granted for many reasons, the most common of which is "appeal on a point of law".[12] In other words, the trial judge erred in not allowing certain evidence to be admitted, in not turning his or her

---

[11] R.S.C. 1985, c. N-5.
[12] Section 839 of the *Criminal Code*.

mind to a particular legal principle, or in not properly instructing the jury. There are, however, several other forms of appeal that are frequently pursued, especially in the criminal justice system, by both the Crown and the accused:

- *Trial de novo*[13] — In summary conviction matters an appeal may be by way of trial *de novo* (literally a "new trial" in a higher court). Often the evidence in the lower court is not taken down by a court reporter so there is no transcript for a court of appeal to review. The only alternative is a new trial.

- *Stated case*[14] — Where the facts are not in dispute but the law is, the party appealing may draft up a "stated case" to be signed by a judge of the trial court. This document is then forwarded to the appeal court where the parties can argue whether the trial judge reached the correct decision on the basis of those facts.

- *Sentence* or *conviction* — In criminal matters an accused person may appeal either the sentence received or the conviction or both. The Crown may also decide that the sentence was not harsh enough or that the accused should have been convicted. It is not uncommon for both parties to appeal simultaneously. For example, an accused may appeal for a lesser sentence at the same time as the Crown Prosecutor appeals on the ground that the sentence was not harsh enough.

CRIMINAL, CIVIL AND LABOUR LAW PRINCIPLES

In this section, we examine the characteristics and differences between criminal, civil and labour law. The underlying principles attached to each are described.

Criminal Law

The objective of criminal law is to protect the public. Revenge is not sought through the criminal law system. With the exception of the rare private prosecution:

- the crime will be investigated by the police;
- a Crown Prosecutor paid by the state will handle the case;
- the case will be prosecuted on behalf of the state, not on behalf of the victim; and

---

[13] Section 822 of the *Criminal Code*.
[14] Sections 829 to 838 of the *Criminal Code*.

- if found guilty, the accused may be required to pay a fine to the government, serve time in a government jail, or report to a government probation officer.

The following chart summarizes the legal powers that security officers, police and prosecutors have in the performance of professional functions.

TABLE OF CRIMINAL LAW POWERS			
	Security	**Police**	**Prosecutor**
Investigation	May investigate	Yes	Not usual
Seizure	Limited	Search under the *Criminal Code*	No
Arrest	Citizen power of arrest	*Criminal Code* and common law power	No
Charge	Private prosecution	Yes	May authorize
Prosecute	Private prosecution	Yes, but seldom exercised	Yes

A criminal offence is generally classified as either a public wrong or a moral wrong.

Public Wrong

Some offences identified by statute are designed simply to protect the public order, for example, statutes that provide for the collection of income, customs or excise taxes. Such statutes were enacted in order to put money into the public coffers. If there were no criminal stigma attached to breaching these laws, many citizens would probably not voluntarily pay their taxes. Another example of a criminal offence covering a public wrong is seat belt legislation. The fact that a person might decide not to wear a seat belt is not in itself a reason for moral outrage: seat belt legislation, however, does address the public's need to lower the health care costs related to driving accidents. The enactment of seat belt legislation has proven to be in the interests of both the individual driver and the public.

Moral Wrong

The other classification of criminal offences comprises those statutes or Acts that have been accepted into law to prohibit conduct that causes harm to members of society. Examples are laws against thefts, assaults and sexual offences, to name the most obvious ones. For some "crimes" in this category, the harm to society is arguably less obvious, although still present. Drug offences and prostitution are often referred to as "victimless crimes", but they are considered so morally reprehensible that statutes were created to control such activities. For better or worse, not all behaviour commonly considered immoral is banned by the criminal statute books.[15] For this reason, an up-to-date knowledge of current legal practice is essential.

Civil Law

Civil actions are initiated to adjust losses and to provide restitution for injuries sustained by a person or corporation as a result of the action or negligence of another. Plaintiffs in civil actions must inform and pay for their own counsel, the court fees and the costs of hiring an investigator where one is required. The procedures for initiating a civil action are quite distinctive such that civil cases are usually heard by judges who uniquely preside over such matters. Where damages are awarded, they are paid to the claimant and not to the state.

Salmond states:[16]

> It is often the case that the same wrong is both civil and criminal — capable of being made the subject of proceedings of both kinds. Assault, libel, theft and malicious injury to property, for example, are wrongs of this kind. Speaking generally, in all such cases the civil and criminal remedies are not alternative but concurrent, each being independent of the other. The wrongdoer may be punished criminally by imprisonment or otherwise and also compelled in a civil action to make compensation or restitution to the injured person.

An interesting bridge between the civil and criminal law has been established in most provinces by criminal injuries compensation boards. These are administrative tribunals set up for the purpose of adjusting losses to the victims of crime, where there is no recourse through civil action. Another bridge between the *Criminal Code* and the civil law is found in section 738 of the *Code*. This section allows a victim to receive compensation for losses by way of an order filed in civil court as a judgment against the accused.

---

[15] Adultery at one time was a *Criminal Code* offence referred to by the courts as "criminal conversation".

[16] Sir John William Salmond (1862-1924) is a well-recognized authority on tort law. See R.F.V. Heuston and R.S. Chambers, *Salmond & Heuston on the Law of Torts,* 19th ed. (London: Sweet & Maxwell, 1987), at p. 9.

Criminal Code Offence	Tort
Theft	Conversion
Assault	Assault or Battery
Trespass	Nuisance
Civil actions in tort often have a criminal counterpart. Torts are rooted in the criminal law because damages are essentially punitive.	

Labour Law

Labour law establishes and enforces the relationships between an employer and an employee. Simultaneous actions may take place from the same set of facts. For example:

1. An employee assaults his supervisor after an argument at the work site following which:
   • he is charged with assault in criminal court;
   • the supervisor initiates a lawsuit to recover damages for medical expenses, lost wages, pain and suffering; and
   • his employment with the company is terminated.
2. Legal actions initiated by the employee may involve:
   • defending himself in criminal court on the assault charge;
   • defending himself in civil court in response to the supervisor's suit to recover damages; or
   • claiming wrongful dismissal in his own civil case (or participating in an arbitration hearing if he is a member of a trade union).

See Chapter 7, "Security and Human Resource Law", for a comprehensive discussion of employment law and relationships and how these affect the performance and responsibilities of security professionals.

The following table summarizes how criminal, civil and labour cases are treated with respect to how they are initiated, the parties involved and the associated legal penalties and awards typically sought.

TABLE OF CRIMINAL, CIVIL AND LABOUR LAW			
	Criminal Law	**Civil Law**	**Labour Law**
Function	public good	private compensation	enforce employment contract
On behalf of	general public	private parties	parties to employment agreement
Handled by	Crown prosecutor	counsel for parties	management/union or their counsel
Result	fine/imprisonment	damages or court order	court or arbitration award

The differences between criminal, civil and labour law may also be seen in the functions of the police and private security.

	Police	**Security**
Employer	the state	private
Function	public prosecution for criminal offences	protect private property
Goal	enforce and investigate	prevent and deter

RESEARCHING THE LAW

Resources

The quality of your research on legal matters depends on the quality of the resources at your disposal. The following materials provide a good starting point for doing legal research. However, you should be aware of the limitations of each type of documentation and take into consideration geographic and historical factors that may impact on the reliability and relevance of the resources you consult.

Textbooks

A variety of legal textbooks is available in Canada. When consulting a textbook, make efficient use of the table of contents and the index. Be cautious if the book was published outside of Canada or deals with non-Canadian legal matters. The development of the law in foreign jurisdictions (even common law jurisdictions) followed unique paths and consequently their statutes will contain numerous differences (often very subtle) when compared to ours.

Encyclopedias and Digests

An excellent source of information is the *Canadian Encyclopedic Digest*.[17] These volumes cover all areas of common, federal and provincial law arranged into hundreds of subject headings. Available in hard copy or as an electronic database, this comprehensive compilation of the law of each of the Canadian jurisdictions is organized by subject titles dealing with specific areas of law. Each title presents statements of law in the form of paragraphs substantiated by one or more footnoted references to case law or legislation. The Digest is intended to be a quick reference and an aid to finding primary sources (*i.e.,* citations of specific laws, regulations and statutes).

The *Canadian Abridgment*[18] provides a digest for all Canadian reported cases (except Quebec civil law cases heard in provincial courts) and many unreported cases. This comprehensive work includes case digests, statute and case citations, a consolidated table of cases and an index to Canadian legal literature. The *Guide to Research Using the Canadian Abridgment* explains how to use this work.

A valuable resource is *Halsbury's Laws of England*.[19] This anthology is organized according to legal topics, identifies British and many Commonwealth cases decided under explicit points of law and has a Canadian converter. A similar anthology, *The Digest*,[20] is also arranged topically, but by contrast provides summaries of British and Commonwealth as well as some European Union and International judgments on points of law.

Statutes and Regulations

At regular intervals every Canadian jurisdiction (federal and provincial) compiles and publishes an up-to-date consolidation of its statutes: *e.g.,* the *Revised Statutes of Canada* (R.S.C.), the *Consolidated Regulations of Canada* (C.R.C.), the *Revised Statutes of Alberta* (R.S.A.), etc. The latest of these consolidations constitute the primary resources for the country's laws and are published by the respective government printers.[21] In addition, each jurisdiction publishes one or more annual statute volumes: *e.g.,* the *2003 Statutes of Canada* (S.C. 2003), containing any

---

17 See *Canadian Encyclopedic Digest Ontario 3rd Edition*, 44 vols., looseleaf (Toronto: Carswell); *Canadian Encyclopedic Digest Western 3rd Edition*, 46 vols., looseleaf (Calgary: Carswell); and *Canadian Encyclopedic Digest On CD-ROM* (Toronto: Carswell).

18 Revised 2nd ed. (Toronto: Carswell, 2002).

19 Now in 4th ed. re-issue (London: Butterworths).

20 (London: Butterworths), regularly updated and re-issued.

21 The last consolidation of Canada's statute law occurred in 1985, thus it is cited as "R.S.C. 1985". A new codification is long overdue.

new Acts and any amendments to existing statutes enacted during that year. Federal and provincial statutes and regulations in their current form may also be accessed over the Internet (*e.g.*, by searching for "Canadian Statutes" on the federal department of Justice Canada or other Internet websites).

For the latest version of a federal regulation, consult the *Canada Gazette Part II*.[22] You can access regulations through the *Gazette*'s quarterly publication "Consolidated Index of Statutory Instruments". This resource contains tables that list the regulations and other statutory instruments (S.I.) alphabetically under the name of the Act whose authority created them.

Provincial statutory instruments can be researched in a similar fashion. Each province publishes official gazettes that contain new regulations and amendments to existing ones. Most provincial regulations are available on the Internet.

Citators and Annotations

A citator is a looseleaf publication that references every statute of a particular jurisdiction, indicating the evolution of every statute section since the last consolidation of statutes was written and identifying any case law that has been argued on any section's point of law. There are many excellent citators available on Canadian law.[23]

Dominion Law Reports Annotations and *Canadian Criminal Cases Annotations* should be consulted as well.[24] These volumes follow the history of published cases showing how often and to what effect the rendered judgments have been used by counsel as supportive precedents (*i.e.*, whether they have been followed, considered, referred to, overturned or distinguished). They also provide brief summaries (catchlines) of numerous points of law upon which judgments were made along with their case cite information.

Law Reports

Dominion Law Reports (D.L.R.) and *Canadian Criminal Cases* (C.C.C.) are examples of law reports. Both publications cover significant federal and provincial judgments from across Canada. These and most other publications have an index to each volume and periodic cumulative indexes. Increasingly, they are also available online.

---

[22] Published by the Queen's Printer, Ottawa.
[23] See: Carswell's *Canadian Abridgement: Canadian Statute Citations* (also on CD-ROM) and *Canadian Abridgement: Canadian Current Law*; Canada Law Book's *Canada Statute Citator*, *Ontario Statute Citator* and *British Columbia Statute Citator* (also on CD-ROM).
[24] Published annually by Canada Law Book, Aurora, Ontario.

Law Reports may be topical (subject-matter oriented), or jurisdictional (report only Supreme Court cases, or Saskatchewan cases, etc.), or regional. Since 1912 *Western Weekly Reports* has covered cases decided in Alberta, British Columbia, Manitoba, the Northwest Territories, Saskatchewan and the Yukon Territory. Cases originating in the maritime provinces of New Brunswick, Newfoundland and Labrador, Nova Scotia and Prince Edward Island were covered by *Eastern Law Reporter* (1905-1914) and *Maritime Provinces Reports* (1929-1968). Since 1975 the *Atlantic Provinces Reports* (A.P.R.) has published only Maritimes cases.

Law reporters were active in pre-Confederation Canada as a glance at the list of Canadian law reports that follows readily attests. Today there are provincial law reporters for every province and territory (Prince Edward Island and Newfoundland have a combined report). Only Ontario and Quebec have had fairly uninterrupted reporting. Links to many recent decisions are available on the Internet.

These are abbreviations for some Canadian reports and their dates of publication:

A.P.R.	*Atlantic Provinces Reports,* 1975 —
Alta. L.R.	*Alberta Law Reports,* 1908-1932, 1977 — (3 series)
A.R.	*Alberta Reports,* 1977 —
B.C.L.R.	*British Columbia Law Reports,* 1977 — (4 series)
B.C.R.	*British Columbia Reports,* 1867-1947
C.C.C.	*Canadian Criminal Cases,* 1893 — (3 series)
C.C.E.L.	*Canadian Cases on Employment Law,* 1983 —
C.H.R.R.	*Canadian Human Rights Reporter,* 1980 —
C.L.R.B.R.	*Canadian Labour Relations Board Reports,* 1974 —
C.R. and	*Criminal Reports* and *Criminal Reports, New*
C.R. (N.S.)	*Series,* 1946 — (6 series)
C.R.R.	*Canadian Rights Reporter,* 1982 — (2 series)
D.L.R.	*Dominion Law Reports,* 1912 — (4 series)
F.C.	*Canada Federal Court Reports,* 1971 —
L.A.C.	*Labour Arbitration Cases,* 1973 — (3 series)
Man. R.	*Manitoba Reports,* 1883-1962, 1979 — (2 series)
M.P.R.	*Maritime Provinces Reports,* 1929-1968
M.V.R.	*Motor Vehicle Reports,* 1978 —
N.B.R.	*New Brunswick Reports,* 1825-1929, 1969 — (2 series)
Nfld. & P.E.I.R.	*Newfoundland and Prince Edward Island Reports,* 1971 —
N.S.R.	*Nova Scotia Reports,* 1834-1929, 1970 — (2 series)
N.W.T.R.	*Northwest Territories Reports,* 1983 —
O.R.	*Ontario Reports,* 1882-1900, 1931 — (3 series)
O.W.N.	*Ontario Weekly Notes,* 1909-1962

Que. C.A., Que. K.B. or Q.B., Que. S.C.	*Quebec Official Reports*, 1892-1985
Q.A.C.	*Quebec Appeal Cases*, 1986 —
R.J.Q.	*Recueil de jurisprudence du Québec*, 1986 —
S.C.R.	*Supreme Court Reports*, 1896 —
Sask. L.R.	*Saskatchewan Law Reports*, 1907-1931
Sask. R.	*Saskatchewan Reports*, 1979 —
W.W.R. and W.W.R. (N.S.)	*Western Weekly Reports* and *Western Weekly Reports, New Series*, 1912 —

Periodicals

Periodicals (journals, law reviews) are published by law schools and other sources. They contain in-depth articles and commentaries on various topics of law. Examples include the *Canadian Business Law Journal*, *Canadian Bar Review* and *McGill Law Review*.

Steps in Legal Research

The following steps should be taken in conducting legal research:

1. Identify the issue that you want to research. Specify key words that may help you when looking through a table of contents or an index.
2. Find a good textbook or two on that area of the law and read the portions of the text that may be of assistance. As you read, make note of cases that seem to be on point.
3. Undertake the same procedures with a legal encyclopedia and note any cases on point.
4. Look up any relevant statutes or regulations. Be aware that there are "annotated" versions of some statutes and that these contain notations about cases that may be helpful.
5. Check for articles in periodicals and commentaries in law reports.
6. Look up the cases that you have determined may be helpful in your research.

Important! Stay objective when doing your research. A search for material that supports only one point of view is dangerous. Read material that supports both sides in order to arrive at a conscious opinion as to the likely outcome. Cases or materials that appear to support your point of view may sometimes turn out to have been "distinguished" (*i.e.,* the legal principle you are interested in was not followed in the case at bar due to a difference in fact or law).

Citation Guide

Before setting out to do legal research it is necessary to understand how citations work; that is, what the numbers and letters are telling you. There are two basic styles used for citations: *volumes in a series* and *volumes in a publication year* (the exceptions are derivatives or foreign reports).[25] Just to complicate things — or so it seems — publishers have at times switched styles, sometimes more than once.

1. *Volumes in a series* — *e.g.,* 3 D.L.R. (4th) 155
- The publisher of the *Dominion Law Reports* (abbreviated as D.L.R.) has numbered the Report's volumes beginning at "1" for the fourth time (4th series). The example above is volume 3 of that series, and the case begins at page 155 in that book.
- Between the names of the parties (*e.g., X v. Y*) and the cite, this style of report citation inserts a year within round brackets that identifies the "year in which the judgment was rendered" followed by a comma. The court that reached the decision follows the cite in abbreviated formula also inside round brackets.
- The whole information will thus appear as:
    e.g., X v. Y (1984), 3 D.L.R. (4th) 155 (Ont. H.C.J.)
    and means that the case of *X v. Y* which was decided in 1984 can be found in the 3rd volume of the 4th series of *Dominion Law Reports* beginning at page 155, which decision was rendered by the Ontario High Court of Justice.
- The 1st series is not identified within brackets:
    e.g., X v. Y (1979), 6 B.C.L.R. 185 (C.A.)

2. *Volumes in a publication year* — *e.g.,* [2000] 2 S.C.R. 307
- The publisher of the *Supreme Court Reports* (S.C.R.) each year produces a number of volumes which are numbered from "1". The example given means that the case cited can be found in the 2nd volume of the production year 2000 beginning at page 307. The year inside the square brackets does *not necessarily* correspond to the year in which the decision was rendered. It could have been decided near the end of 1999, for example.
- In this style the square bracketed year is *part of* the cite and thus is preceded by a comma. The whole information would be given as:
    e.g., X v. Y, [2000] 2 S.C.R. 307

---

[25] Later in the book several United States cases are referenced. Their format looks different but the same principles apply: front number represents the volume; back number represents the page; in-between is the law report abbreviation (F., F.2d, F.3d refer to the *Federal Reporter* of the 1st, 2nd, or 3rd series; U.S. stands for the *United States Reports* which only report United States Supreme Court judgments); followed by the judgment year in round brackets.

- Note that the court information (S.C.C.) is unnecessary here because S.C.R. *only* reports cases from the Supreme Court of Canada.
- Note also that when only one volume is produced in the publication year the cite will be given without a volume number:

  e.g., X v. Y, [1975] F.C. 587

When a case is referenced in a judgment or other text, it is often accompanied by additional information. There may be parallel cites (indicating that the case was reported by more than one publisher), or a history of the case through various stages of appeal may be provided. The words "affd" (affirmed) or "revd" (reversed) indicate that the decision was either upheld or overturned by a higher court. The decision may also have been "vard" (varied) meaning part of it was upheld, part was not.

CONCLUSION

Owing to the complexity of the Canadian legal system it is important to understand the basic principles under which our system operates. The use of precedent (the idea that courts must stand by their past judgments) is a key element in Canadian law. Our court system, constitutional law, public law and private law, as they have evolved, have all contributed to the Canadian legal mosaic. An understanding and awareness of how laws are interpreted and in what context they are considered are the key success factors for those working in the private security area. The impact of privacy rights, human rights, Charter rights and labour legislation on security operations will be explored further in the succeeding chapters.

2
Human Rights

INTRODUCTION

When we think about human rights, we are thinking about global human values. These values are common currency in our everyday lives: our standards of behaviour in the workplace, as well as socially, are based on the principles of fairness set down in human rights legislation. If racism, sexism, religious persecution and age discrimination were not evident in modern life, there would be no need for human rights legislation. It is important, then, to appreciate that because security work involves people, a basic knowledge and understanding of the fundamental rules, rights and protections afforded to all members of society is essential.

HUMAN RIGHTS PROTECTIONS BY LAW

In 1948, the United Nations adopted the *Universal Declaration of Human Rights*[1] to guarantee basic human rights. Article 1 of the Declaration proclaimed: "All human beings are born free and equal in dignity and rights." Article 2 asserted: "Everyone is entitled to all the rights and freedoms set forth in this Declaration, without distinction of any kind, such as race, colour, sex, language, religion, political or other opinion, national or social origin, property, birth or other status." These two articles constitute the basic tenets of federal and provincial human rights legislation in Canada. Protection of these rights in Canada is further guaranteed in federal and provincial statutes.

---

[1] General Assembly Resolution 217, adopted December 10, 1948.

Federal Statutes

The *Canadian Bill of Rights*[2] became law in Canada in 1960 and provided a guideline for the application of human rights law. However, because it was in essence only the federal government's statement of intent to apply the United Nations' protections, it was not entrenched in the same manner as the United States' *Bill of Rights*.[3] As a result, it was rarely used in the determination of civil or criminal matters in court.

The *Canadian Human Rights Act*[4] was passed in 1977 and provided the legal means for safeguarding and enforcing human rights. The statute is regulatory and stipulates what constitutes offences and the fines or other penalties for non-compliance. Included is the provision for review by the Canadian Human Rights Commission of cases brought before it. Because it is a federal statute, it has jursidiction only within the domain of the federal government and, as such, applies specifically to:

- departments and agencies of the federal government;
- Crown corporations; and
- businesses governed by federal jurisdiction (*e.g.*, banks, airlines and railways).

The *Canadian Human Rights Act* prohibits discriminatory practices based on:

- race
- national or ethnic origin
- colour
- religion
- age
- sex
- sexual orientation
- marital status
- family status
- disability
- conviction for an offence for which a pardon has been granted.

Later amendments to the statute provided for the protection of personal information and access to information in federal files and records.

Provincial Statutes

Although they vary slightly from province to province, the provincial statutes (referred to variously as the *Human Rights Code, Human Rights*

---

[2]   S.C. 1960, c. 44, or see R.S.C. 1985, Appendix III.
[3]   Amendments 1 to 10 of the United States Constitution.
[4]   S.C. 1976-77, c. 33 (now R.S.C. 1985, c. H-6).

Act or *Individual Rights Protection Act*) generally prohibit discrimination in:

- property rights (purchase and tenancy); and
- employment (wages, hiring and the right to belong to employee associations).

In addition, they provide for a tribunal to investigate, hear complaints and enforce the legislation. Some statutes also provide sanctions against hate literature.

Human rights legislation generally takes precedence over other rights. No individual or entity can simply contract away the rights or obligations the legislation imposes. An individual who believes that he or she has been discriminated against may take action by lodging a complaint with the appropriate human rights commission or tribunal. The complaint is then investigated and reported upon before the commission determines whether it will be pursued via legal action.

Not only are individuals becoming more informed and cognizant of their fundamental rights, but the need for respecting them within the framework of business operations is increasingly evident. In a 1992 Ontario case, a company was downsizing and laid off an older supervisor while keeping a younger one. Rather than sue for wrongful dismissal, the laid-off employee complained to the Ontario Human Rights Commission. His case was successful and his award was his salary from age 57 (when he was terminated) to age 65 (when he would normally have retired). This amount was significantly larger than he would have received if his notice period had simply been increased.[5]

MEETING HUMAN RIGHTS REQUIREMENTS

Human rights, Charter rights and privacy rights must be understood and applied appropriately in the course of business operations. To work effectively, security professionals need to know how to answer questions, such as:

- Can an employee be terminated for having a criminal conviction?
- Can an employer legally search an employee's locker, personal effects and computer desktop without infringing personal rights?
- Under what circumstances can an interrogation occur in the workplace?

Such questions will be explored in detail in this and later chapters.

---

[5]   *Hayes-Dana Inc. v. McKee* (1992), 17 C.H.R.R. D/79, 92 C.L.L.C. ¶17,029 (Ont. Bd. Inq.).

Human rights legislation is having more and more of an impact on our society and must be paid careful attention by every corporation in the way it does business. In the performance of their duties (*e.g.*, investigative work, background research), security professionals need to avoid any approach that might be considered or perceived to be discriminatory in nature. Working with corporate management, they must ensure that proper procedures are followed and that fairness principles are observed. Two areas are especially relevant:

1. *Hiring standards* — Corporations must act responsibly and avoid unfair hiring practices. (For more information on occupational law and policies, refer to Chapter 7, "Security and Human Resource Law".)
2. *Conduct during internal investigations* — The conduct of an internal investigation is one of the most crucial tasks of a security department. The security investigator must ensure that the rights of the employee to confidentiality, the rights of the corporation to a thorough assessment of the facts and the proper protection of evidence are properly balanced. A model for internal investigations is provided in Chapter 7.

Harassment

Harassment falls within the provisions of both federal and provincial human rights legislation. Some legislation specifically addresses the issue of harassment while in other statutes it is covered under the grounds of discrimination. Specifically, sexual harassment is unwelcome behaviour that is sexual in nature and, directly or indirectly, adversely affects or threatens to affect a person's job security, his or her prospects for promotion or earnings and the workplace attitude and conditions that surround him or her. Harassment is an attempt by one person to exercise perceived power over another.

Federal and Provincial Legal Frameworks re Harassment

It is instructive for our purposes to look at a key section of the *Canadian Human Rights Act*. Section 14 states:

> 14(1) It is a discriminatory practice,
>> (*a*)   in the provision of goods or services, facilities or accommodation customarily available to the general public,
>> (*b*)   in the provision of commercial premises or residential accommodation, or
>> (*c*)   in matters related to employment,
> to harass an individual on a prohibited ground of discrimination.
>
> (2) Without limiting the generality of subsection (1), sexual harassment shall, for the purposes of that subsection, be deemed to be harassment on a prohibited ground of discrimination.

The federal statute and some of the provincial statutes have provisions that specifically mention sexual harassment. In those provincial statutes that do not call attention to sexual harassment, the unwanted behaviour is prohibited under the ground of gender discrimination. In the Province of Ontario, sexual harassment has moreover been accepted as a health and safety issue; hence, an aggrieved person can apply to the Labour Relations Board and/or the Workers' Compensation Board for damages.

The official complaint process varies from jurisdiction to jurisdiction but, generally speaking, the process provides for:

- a signed complaint within a specified time;
- legal notification of the respondent and a chance to respond to the complaint;
- a conciliation process;
- an investigative process; and
- an adjudication.

The relevant commissions have very broad powers to award damages and/or order the respondent company to create compliant policies, provide training and/or undertake other appropriate measures.

Any act of harassment committed by an employee or agent of an employer in the course of the employment could be considered an act committed by the employer. Therefore, an employer might find itself liable for acts of harassment occurring either at or away from the work site both during or after normal working hours, provided that the acts were committed "within the course of employment". The term "within the course of employment" will obviously be difficult to define in many cases and often there are shades of grey in the interpretation of the term.

In one unreported federal case, two government employees were assigned to go out of town to attend some seminars. A female employee was booked into a bedroom attached to the hotel hospitality suite that was used for the after-hours entertainment of the participants. The female employee afterwards alleged that she had been harassed by her superior between 2 and 3 a.m. The adjudicating tribunal ruled that it did not have jurisdiction in the case because the matter occurred outside the scope of employment. This ruling was upheld by a federal court. It should be noted that this decision did not preclude the complainant from pursuing a civil action against the harasser, even though it indicated that the employer was not responsible for the act of harassment.

Another case brought before the Supreme Court of Canada challenged the amount of time required to investigate a complaint in a harassment action, alleging consequential human rights infringement. The Supreme Court of Canada addressed the question of whether a harassment complaint could be thrown out because of a delay in the time for investigating the complaint. In *Blencoe v. British Columbia (Human Rights*

Commission)[6] the complaint had languished with the Human Rights Commission for 33 months before being scheduled for a hearing. Mr. Blencoe argued that the review should be terminated because his rights under section 7 of the Charter (the right to life, liberty and security of the person) had been breached. The Supreme Court of Canada held that whereas section 7 did apply to human rights proceedings, there had been no denial of life, liberty and security of the person. The Commission had placed no constraints on Mr. Blencoe's ability to make decisions and therefore his rights to life and liberty were not infringed. The Supreme Court ordered that an expedited hearing take place before the British Columbia Human Rights Commission with costs against the Commission to compensate for the delay.

Definition of Sexual Harassment

Most human rights organizations define sexual harassment broadly in terms of:

- verbal abuse or threats;
- unwelcome remarks, jokes, innuendoes or taunting about a person's body, attire, age, marital status, ethnic or national origin, religion, etc.;
- the display of pornographic, racist or other offensive or derogatory images;
- practical jokes that cause awkwardness or embarrassment;
- unwelcome invitations or requests, whether indirect or explicit, or intimidation;
- leering or other gestures;
- condescension or paternalism that undermines self-respect;
- unnecessary physical contact such as touching, patting, pinching, punching; and
- physical assault.

There are two main types of workplace sexual harassment:

1. *Quid pro quo* — A demand of sexual favours for a right or benefit of work. "Go along with me or you won't get hired, a day off, promotion, transfer, etc."
2. *Environment* — Sometimes referred to as a "poisoned work environment", this form of sexual harassment involves improper verbal or physical conduct of a sexual nature, unwanted comments, the visual display of degrading or demeaning pictures, or unwanted sexual advances or contact. Often, in this type of harassment, many people are participating in the objectionable activity.

---

[6]   (2000), 190 D.L.R. (4th) 513, [2000] 2 S.C.R. 307.

Sexual harassment may be:	It may:
• verbal • physical • deliberate • unsolicited • unwelcome in the eyes of a reasonable person • one incident or a series of incidents	• be reasonably perceived as a term or condition of employment (*i.e.*, its availability or continuation), or the provision of goods, services, accommodation, etc. • influence decisions on the above items • interfere with job performance or access to goods, services, etc. • humiliate, insult or intimidate any individual

To summarize, sexual harassment is unwelcome sexual behaviour that threatens to affect a person's job security, working conditions and/or economic potential in employment.

Costly Consequences

Workplace misbehaviour involving human rights violations, such as sexual harassment, is expensive. The associated costs include:

- legal liability and penalties
- settlements
- investigations
- labour relations issues
- decreased productivity
- absenteeism
- stress-related illness
- turnover and instability
- poor morale
- damage to corporate public image.

Human Rights and Criminal Convictions

It is a common misconception that an employer cannot ask whether a potential employee has suffered a past criminal conviction, or refuse to hire or refuse to continue to employ someone who has been found guilty of a criminal offence. The federal statute does provide that such refusal is grounds for discrimination where a pardoned offence appears on a personal record. Most provincial statutes are mute on the point and some (*e.g.*, British Columbia) simply provide a ground for discrimination where the criminal offence does not relate to employment.

A provision like the one in the British Columbia statute can create some interesting problems for the employer. It would be fairly easy to argue when hiring for a security position that a conviction for theft must relate to employment since the applicant or incumbent is expected to protect the property of others. Often, however, the correlation between the criminal conviction and the job is not very clear, and the employer must be in a position to defend its decision before a human rights tribunal.

Employers are continually faced with human rights dilemmas: in one unreported British Columbia case, a male worker at a drug manufacturing firm was charged with a sexual assault on a female employee after working hours. The employer could not terminate the male employee because the conviction was pending and because the grounds needed to argue that the offence of sexual assault related to employment were not strong. The union threatened job action if the employer did not remove the male employee from the job site; at the same time, the employee threatened to go before a human rights tribunal if he was removed from his job. The company's response to resolve the issue was to put the employee on administrative suspension with pay until the criminal trial. He was convicted and sentenced to jail, then terminated by the company with the union's compliance for being absent without leave.

Drug Testing and Investigations

Introduction

Substance abuse investigations require particular care in handling. For this reason, they will be described here in some detail. They also provide a good illustration of the relationship between responsible human rights practices and investigative professionalism.

From a legal standpoint, it is interesting to begin by noting that there is no legislation in place federally or in any of the provinces that either requires or authorizes a workplace drug program.[7] The decision to test employees for drugs is not one that is taken lightly or without a great deal of input from many parts of an organization. For this reason, many large Canadian corporations have developed comprehensive substance-abuse programs, some of which involve drug testing. The decision to implement a drug-testing program may be based on several factors:

- a history of drug-related incidents in the corporation;
- the nature of the industry and the number of safety-sensitive jobs;

---

[7]   The federal government has considered legislation requiring drug testing for certain occupations in the transportation industry: see *Strategy on Substance Use in Safety-Sensitive Positions in Canadian Transportation* (Ottawa: Transport Canada, March, 1990). Similar legislation exists in the United States in the form of the Department of Transport Federal Highway Administration Regulations, with which, as of July, 1997, Canadian truckers traveling into the United States must comply.

- the fact that service-related industries may be more likely to consider drug testing as a result of pressure from their clients;
- the overall maturity of the employee population — a company in which the average age of employees is relatively young is more likely to experience problems than a corporation with a more mature population;
- the overall bias of senior management towards drugs;
- the likelihood of acceptance by the employee population of the program; and
- the corporation's perception of how such testing will be supported in future legislation and how the law will be applied by the courts, as well as by labour or human rights tribunals.

When deciding whether to implement mandatory testing, a company needs to first consider the extent of the problem and whether it is willing to bear the costs associated with the pursuit of disciplinary action following the discovery of a positive test result. The cost of the individual tests is a small part of the total costs of such a program. For example, there may be costs related to flying the medical team into remote locations to administer the tests, to establishing which jobs within the organization are safety sensitive and to administering the program in the long term. In addition, the employer must consider what effects such a program and its implementation will have on the workplace.

Federal and provincial statutes do not specifically prohibit drug testing but human rights commissions and tribunals have tended to interpret the "disability" sections of the statutes to include discrimination based on the disability of addiction to alcohol or drugs. An example is the federal Canadian Human Rights Commission's position, which is described in a following section.

Drug-testing Definitions

The following are important terms in the area of drug testing:

1. *Pre-employment* — Mandatory testing of either every potential employee or every candidate for identified positions as a condition of employment. Candidates may refuse the test but usually will not be considered for employment.
2. *Random* — Irregular testing of the employee population or some portion of it (*e.g.*, identified safety-sensitive jobs).
3. *Mandatory-universal* — All employees are tested.
4. *For cause testing* — Mandatory testing where there is reasonable evidence that an employee is influenced by alcohol or drugs or following an accident or near miss incident.
5. *Reinstatement testing* — Testing following a disciplinary or administrative suspension for a breach of the drug policy.

6. *Consent* — Testing only after an employee or applicant has provided consent (usually written).
7. *Blanket* — Testing of all employees or occupations regardless of the sensitivity of the position.

The Federal Jurisdiction

The Canadian Human Rights Commission ("C.H.R.C.") promulgated a policy as early as 1988 outlining its position on drug testing.[8] Specific policy statements are described below:

1. Mass and random testing should not be implemented and individual tests should only be considered when performance deficiencies have been observed. When the employer cannot identify deficiencies by performance evaluation, drug testing for that position may be permissible if being drug free is essential to safe work performance.
2. Pre-employment or random screening should only be considered when an individual's job poses a safety risk and where the individual's behavior cannot be observed.
3. The purpose of drug screening should only be to refer employees to an employee assistance program.
4. The C.H.R.C. will deal with complaints where an individual alleges discrimination on the basis of disability, sex, age or race as a result of a requirement to undergo a mandatory drug test or as a result of a positive drug test.
5. The C.H.R.C. accepts the premise that there may be a correlation between the results of drug tests and job performance in which case the C.H.R.C. must consider the *bona fide* occupational requirement ("BFOR") argument:
    *   the employer must establish that the practice requires that the individual have the capacity to perform the essential components of the job safely, efficiently and reliably;
    *   the employer must generally assess each individual's capacity to perform safely, efficiently and reliably and must do so in an accurate and valid manner;
    *   the employer must, where reasonably possible, avoid any discriminatory effect on the individual.
6. The C.H.R.C. will adopt the procedures outlined by the Addiction Research Foundation as being the minimum standard required for tests to provide accurate, valid and confidential results.

---

[8] "Policy 88-1, Drug Testing" (Ottawa: Canadian Human Rights Commission, 1988).

7. The C.H.R.C. will determine, in accordance with the facts of each case, whether the employer has a duty to provide reasonable accommodation or whether an action taken constitutes reasonable accommodation.

In assessing any policy that may be discriminatory (*e.g.*, drug testing, harassment, hiring policies, etc.), a court or human rights commission will use the following analysis.

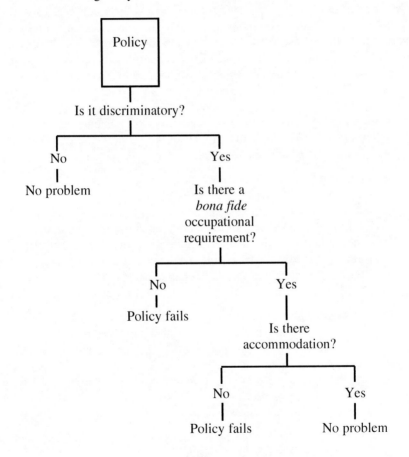

The first question the court will ask is: "Is the policy discriminatory?" There is a common misconception that policies must not discriminate. In some cases, discrimination is legally justifiable. An advertisement in the newspaper that states "No females need apply" is an example of direct discrimination, but the discrimination may be legally justifiable if the position is to play the lead role in *Hamlet* or to act as a cleaner in a men's locker room.

Bona Fide Occupational Requirement (BFOR)

As indicated earlier, discrimination may be legally appropriate if there is a *bona fide* occupational requirement. The courts will be much more willing to accept that an airline pilot must not be addicted to drugs or alcohol than that a clerk in a non-safety sensitive position must not be so addicted. Because *bona fide* occupational requirements may be scrutinized, such decisions to discriminate according to the nature of the work must be carefully taken and they must also be legally defensible. Tawney Meiorin was a British Columbia firefighter who was terminated in 1994 when she failed a test to run 2.5 kilometers in 11 minutes or less. She alleged discrimination on the basis of sex because men and women have different aerobic capacity and she brought her case to the Supreme Court of Canada.[9] In 1999 the Supreme Court ruled in her favour: she was rewarded five years of back pay and reinstated in her firefighter job. The Supreme Court of Canada held that in order to justify an employment rule or policy that is *prima facie* discriminatory, employers and others must show on a balance of probabilities that:

- the standard is adopted for a purpose or goal that is rationally connected to the function being performed;
- the standard is adopted in good faith, in the belief that it is necessary for the fulfilment of the legitimate purpose or goal; and
- the standard is reasonably necessary to accomplish its purpose or goal, in the sense that the employer cannot accommodate persons with the characteristics of the claimant without incurring undue hardship.

The court held that it was not demonstrated that the test in this case was a *bona fide* occupational requirement for the job. The employer must ensure that, if there are requirements for a job, they are related to the ability to do the job.

Because there have not been a large number of Canadian cases on the topic, we must look to some U.S. cases for definitions of safety sensitivity. Three such definitions follow:

- "a clear nexus . . . between the nature of the employee's duty and the nature of the feared violation";[10]
- positions in which individuals discharged "duties fraught with such risks of injury to others that even a momentary lapse of attention can have disastrous consequences";[11]

---

[9] *British Columbia (Public Service Employee Relations Commission) v. B.C.G.E.U.* (1999), 176 D.L.R. (4th) 1, [1999] 3 S.C.R. 3 ("*Meiorin*"), at para. 54.

[10] *Harmon v. Thornburgh*, 878 F.2d 484 (D.C. Cir. 1989).

[11] *Skinner v. Railway Labor Executives' Assn.*, 489 U.S. 602 (1989), at p. 628.

- "the most salient factor in determining the safety-sensitivity of a job is the immediacy of the threat posed to the public by an employee whose judgment and perception is impaired by drug and alcohol use".[12]

An example of a U.S. case where the test for a BFOR passed scrutiny is one in which a court clerk altered computer data (*i.e.*, criminal records); however, in a different case, a U.S. court held that there was no BFOR where a court clerk had access to drugs but was under supervision.

Accommodation

The next consideration by the court or commission in determining if there has been discrimination is whether the employer met a duty to accommodate the employee:[13]

> . . . where a rule has an adverse discriminatory effect, the appropriate response is to uphold the rule in its general application and consider whether the employer could have accommodated the employee adversely affected without undue hardship.

In many of the pre-employment drug testing cases, the duty to accommodate was met by offering the applicant employee assistance counseling. In a case involving the Toronto Dominion Bank:[14]

1. An applicant was first offered employment, subject to a negative test.
2. If the test result was positive, the applicant was given probationary employment for 30 days and employee assistance counseling.
3. At the end of 30 days, a subsequent test was given.
4. If the results were negative, the probationary employee was hired.
5. If the results were positive, a further 30 days of counseling were prescribed.
6. At the end of the second 30-day period, upon testing positive, the probationary employee was terminated.

---

[12] *Kemp v. Clairborne County Hospital*, 763 F.Supp. 1362 (S.D. Miss. 1991).

[13] *Central Alberta Dairy Pool v. Alberta (Human Rights Commission)* (1990), 72 D.L.R. (4th) 417, [1990] 2 S.C.R. 489.

[14] *Canadian Civil Liberties Assn. v. Toronto Dominion Bank* (1994), 6 C.C.E.L. (2d) 196, 22 C.H.R.R. D/301 (Can. Trib.), quashed 22 C.C.E.L. (2d) 229, 25 C.H.R.R. D/301 (F.C.T.D.), affd 163 D.L.R. (4th) 193, [1998] 4 F.C. 205 (C.A.). The tribunal had ruled that the drug testing policy adopted by the bank was justifiable and dismissed the complaint. The C.H.R.C. applied for judicial review of the tribunal's decision and it was set aside by a motions judge of the trial court. The bank appealed to the Federal Court of Appeal. One of the bank's arguments was that employees who have alcohol or drug dependency would be more susceptible to influence from organized crime.

It is important that the offer of employment be made prior to the test in order to demonstrate that the company is not discriminating and that it is, in fact, offering the job to the best candidate and not simply to someone who can pass the drug-screening test.

If the employer has met the duty to accommodate, the court or commission will then consider whether there is a connection in the case between substance abuse and job performance (BFOR).

Core Principles to Deter Drug and Alcohol Abuse

Core principles of any substance-abuse program should include:

1. An employer does not have an unlimited duty to accommodate an employee who refuses to participate in rehabilitation.[15]
2. There is no requirement that the employee who suffers from addiction must also exhibit poor job performance.
3. The *Canadian Charter of Rights and Freedoms* does not apply to private parties (*e.g.*, right to privacy).
4. No one may contract out of the human rights legislation.
5. It is discriminatory for employers to require employees to disclose past alcohol abuse.[16]
6. It is discriminatory to remove an employee from a safety-sensitive position when he or she is a recovering alcoholic.

Standards for Employers

An employer challenged on a drug-testing policy must be prepared to establish the following factors:

1. A link or nexus exists between the positive test and the capacity to meet the job requirements.
2. There must be demonstrable evidence that, because of the nature of the risk in the job or the lack of ability to supervise and observe the worker, drug screening is considered necessary.
3. Mass or random testing should be avoided.
4. Drug testing may be considered where there is evidence of job performance deficiencies and where the behaviour constitutes a risk. The testing should include a referral to a qualified medical practitioner.
5. Tests must be conducted in a reliable manner.

---

[15] *Niles v. Canadian National Railway Co.* (1992), 94 D.L.R. (4th) 33, 18 C.H.R.R. D/152 (Ont. C.A.).

[16] *Entrop v. Imperial Oil Ltd.* (2000), 189 D.L.R. (4th) 14, 2 C.C.E.L. (3d) 19 (Ont. C.A.).

Administering the Test

The Addiction Research Foundation has outlined the following steps to ensure "valid, accurate and confidential results" for corporations that are contemplating the development and implementation of a drug-testing program:

1. Samples should be collected by qualified staff under medical supervision and forwarded to a qualified laboratory.
2. The individual being tested should have the right to provide and should have recorded a statement of current medical or other drug use.
3. All positive results should be confirmed by chromatography/mass spectrometry.
4. The laboratory should not forward positive results unless the results have been confirmed by this method.
5. The laboratory should communicate test results only to the licensed medical practitioner who forwarded the test samples to the laboratory.
6. The practitioner should report back to the employee on the results of the testing and his/her interpretation in accordance with standard medical ethics and applicable company policies and agreements.

In addition, the employer should ensure that the tests are specifically oriented to the ability of the employee or candidate to perform the job effectively and safely. The employer should also consider preventive measures, including written policies that clearly state the consequences of impairment while in the workplace (up to and including termination). An employee assistance program is a key component of any substance-abuse program and should also be available.

The Privacy Commissioner who is responsible for applying the federal *Privacy Act*[17] has expressed the opinion that random, mandatory drug testing would infringe the Act. Those provincial and federal jurisdictions that have established policies relating to drug testing have done so by interpreting the proscribed ground of "disability" in their statutes as including past or present dependency and perceived dependency on drugs or alcohol. Boards and commissions make no distinction between legal and illegal drugs.

The extensive development of drug-testing programs by organizations in the United States has caused many Canadian companies and the federal government to look at adopting similar programs here. Criminal problems as well as culture and the legal system are different in Canada, however, and the idea of drug testing has not been as readily accepted by labour and human rights groups. Before embarking on a drug-testing program, a Canadian organization must address:

---

[17] R.S.C. 1985, c. P-21.

- procedures where there is a positive test;
- the likelihood of winning a challenge to a drug-testing policy for a refusal to take the test or a disciplinary action following a positive test;
- the extensive costs that may be involved;
- whether there is an existing drug problem or whether this is simply a reaction to media perception of a drug problem; and
- whether any apparent problem can better be handled with supervisory training and employee assistance programs and investigations.

The Substance Abuse Tool Kit

The employer can adopt a number of means to reduce substance abuse in the workplace. They include:

- policy
- drug and alcohol testing
- employee assistance programs
- investigation
- training and awareness.

Each of these areas is discussed in the following sections of this chapter.

Policy

Any policy that is created should:

- be appropriate to the need;
- be clear and concise;
- set out expectations;
- define responsibilities;
- define consequences; and
- meet legal requirements.

A policy can have a number of benefits, including communicating expectations to employees, acting as a vehicle for discussion, establishing a method to research the issues and providing credibility in the event of litigation and arbitration. A policy should contain prohibitions on the sale, use, transfer and/or possession of illicit drugs or alcohol and associated impairment. It should also address testing and confidentiality issues and be able to stand up to legal challenges.

Drug and alcohol testing

The *Entrop* decision,[18] for example, at the Ontario Court of Appeal not only confirmed that alcohol and drug abuse are to be treated as handicaps,

---

[18]   *Supra*, footnote 16.

but that a positive drug test does not indicate impairment, only the presence of alcohol or drugs. The court did hold, however, that "for cause" drug testing might be permitted following an accident or incident and post-reinstatement testing might be permitted. The court also made note of the fact that a breathalyzer test could show present impairment and might be permissible at the work site. Imperial Oil's policy that required those with an alcohol or drug addiction to declare themselves was ruled against by the court in this decision because it failed the third test in *Meiorin*.

Employee assistance programs

An employee assistance program is an integral part of the tool kit because it adds credibility and ensures that the program's intended effects meet human rights requirements. Employee assistance counselors play an important role in every phase of a drug and alcohol rehabilitation program, from providing counseling to employees who undertake self-referral because of their concern for addiction, to assisting supervisors in dealing with performance issues related to addiction and to an employee's return to work following referral to a clinic.

Investigation

Investigation provides a deterrent to substance abuse and helps to establish the root cause and extent of the problem. Thorough investigations will also decrease liability and assist in litigation and arbitration.

Substance abuse investigations often reveal that there was a long-term problem within a work site — that a substance abuse organization existed at the workplace with major and minor dealers and users. Often co-workers are aware of the problem and wonder why management is doing nothing about it, while managers and supervisors may be surprised at the extent of the problem. That problem may include illicit drugs, licit drugs and alcohol.

Training and awareness

Training programs serve as due diligence in getting the message out to employees that drug abuse will not be tolerated. The steps in creating a training program are:

- identify the need ("needs assessment");
- determine training content;
- identify who should be trained;
- analyze the return on training investment; and
- establish a budget and make available or identify qualified trainers and/or training technologies.

Training objectives should include an awareness of the policy, an awareness of the problem and the establishment of accountability.

CONCLUSION

This chapter presented information on human rights protections in Canada. The federal and provincial statutes governing human rights were introduced, as well as the need for organizations and security people to ensure that human rights are respected at all times. Whether performing background checks on potential employees, investigating unacceptable employee behaviour, or protecting enterprises from commercial threat, security people need to know how to work within the intent of human rights legislation.

3

The Canadian Charter of Rights and Freedoms

INTRODUCTION

Unlike the law in the United States, where the Constitution guarantees basic inalienable rights of the individual, such rights have been established in Canada, as in Great Britain, through common law principles that protect the rights of individual citizens.

In 1982, the federal government enacted the *Canadian Charter of Rights and Freedoms* at the same time as it repatriated the Canadian Constitution. The Charter was passed in order to entrench the common law rights to freedom of speech and freedom of religion, to prohibit discrimination in all of its forms and to ensure that no person in Canada is subjected to cruel and unusual punishment or treatment.

TRUTH AND FAIRNESS

The ideals of truth and fairness are continuously at odds in the criminal justice process. Often it is impossible for the courts to arrive at a decision as to whether an accused is guilty or innocent (the truth) without infringing upon the rights of that person (fairness). In spite of the fact that the "golden thread" woven into our system holds that an accused is innocent until proven guilty,[1] the law allows the police to infringe upon the rights that an accused would normally have if he or she had not been accused of an offence. The police may arrest, search and detain the individual, take fingerprints and DNA samples and search the home with the acquisition of a search warrant, all before an accused has been proven guilty.

The question is: "How far should the police be allowed to go in infringing on the rights of an accused in order to ensure that the court is presented

---

[1] *Woolmington v. Director of Public Prosecutions*, [1935] A.C. 462 (H.L.).

45

with all of the evidence?" That question is a difficult one and there is no definitive answer. We can say that basically the United States system leans towards "fairness", while the Canadian criminal justice system favours the "truth" part of the equation.

As an illustration of the difference between the two approaches, it has always been held in Canada that a confession by an accused may not be admitted into evidence if it has been improperly obtained (by threats or promises). This common law principle arose from the Judges' Rules set into practice in Great Britain. The issue is not, as it is in the United States, that the police must act fairly or that they must not beat a confession out of the accused; rather, it is a question of truth: Was the confession the truth or was it given to stop the abuse?

The predilection in favour of truth in the Canadian criminal court system is illustrated by a 1970 Supreme Court of Canada decision. In *R. v. Wray*[2] the accused was placed under investigation by the Ontario Provincial Police for the murder of a service station attendant during a hold-up near Peterborough, Ontario. The police interrogated the suspect for some time and finally, after intense questioning, he led the police to the location where the murder weapon had been discarded. During the trial, the judge ruled that the confession had not been voluntary because of the length of the interrogation. That ruling was upheld on appeal. Furthermore, the trial judge had ruled that because the confession was not voluntary all evidence pertaining to the locating of the murder weapon was also inadmissible because its admission would operate unfairly against the accused. The Ontario Court of Appeal upheld the trial judge's decision that the evidence must be excluded if its admissibility could be "calculated to bring the administration of justice into disrepute" (because of unfairness to the accused). The Supreme Court of Canada, however, held that no such doctrine existed in Canadian law, overturned the decisions of the Court of Appeal and the trial court and ordered a new trial. Mr. Justice Martland of the Supreme Court of Canada stated:[3]

> The allowance of admissible evidence relevant to the issue before the Court and of substantial probative value may operate unfortunately for the accused, but not unfairly.

Thus, Canada had been placed squarely on the "truth" side of the pendulum.

---

[2]　(1970), 11 D.L.R. (3d) 673, [1970] 4 C.C.C. 1 (S.C.C.), revg [1970] 3 C.C.C. 122, 9 C.R. (N.S.) 131 (Ont. C.A.).

[3]　*Supra*, at p. 689.

Section 24 of the Charter

Parliament, in its wisdom, may have decided that the Supreme Court of Canada was right in its interpretation of the law, but as far as our legislators were concerned that was not the way the law ought to be. When the *Canadian Charter of Rights and Freedoms* was passed in 1982, section 24 provided:

> 24(1) Anyone whose rights or freedoms, as guaranteed by this Charter, have been infringed or denied may apply to a court of competent jurisdiction to obtain such remedy as the court considers appropriate and just in the circumstances.
>
> (2) Where, in proceedings under subsection (1), a court concludes that evidence was obtained in a manner that infringed or denied any rights or freedoms guaranteed by this Charter, the evidence shall be excluded if it is established that, having regard to all the circumstances, the admission of it in the proceedings would bring the administration of justice into disrepute.

The courts were suddenly vested with the power to exclude evidence, which was "fruit of the poisoned tree". Civil rights activists across the country saw this as the introduction of a new golden age for human rights in Canada. Prosecutors and the police saw it as an "Americanization" of the criminal law that would throw open the jailhouse doors as a result of the slightest flaw in the police investigation. Judges in Canada quickly established, however, that if there were any change at all it would not be significant. In a fairly early decision by the Ontario Court of Appeal, Mr. Justice Zuber stated:[4]

> In view of the number of cases in Ontario trial courts in which Charter provisions are being argued, and especially in view of some of the bizarre and colourful arguments being advanced, it may be appropriate to observe that the Charter does not intend a transformation of our legal system or the paralysis of law enforcement. Extravagant interpretation can only trivialize and diminish respect for the Charter, which is a part of the supreme law of this country.

The Charter has served to validate human rights in Canada as they were formulated by the common law. The Supreme Court has indicated that its interpretation of the Charter will remain firmly on the truth side of the equation.

Note that the Charter does not provide for fines, sentences or other forms of discipline, and the only sanction or penalty that results from a breach of the Charter is that evidence may be excluded from admission in court if its introduction offends the intent of the statute. The main differ-

---

4   *R. v. Altseimer* (1982), 142 D.L.R. (3d) 246 at p. 252, 1 C.C.C. (3d) 7 (Ont. C.A.).

ence between the Charter and federal and provincial human rights legislation is that the latter provides for punishment.

Rights Under the Charter

The following rights are guaranteed in sections 7 to 14 of the *Canadian Charter of Rights and Freedoms*:

Life, Liberty and Security of Person

7. Everyone has the right to life, liberty and security of the person and the right not to be deprived thereof except in accordance with the principles of fundamental justice.

Search or Seizure

8. Everyone has the right to be secure against unreasonable search and seizure.

Detention or Imprisonment

9. Everyone has the right not to be arbitrarily detained or imprisoned.

Arrest or Detention

10. Everyone has the right on arrest or detention
    (*a*)   to be informed promptly of the reasons therefor;
    (*b*)   to retain and instruct counsel without delay and to be informed of that right; and
    (*c*)   to have the validity of the detention determined by way of *habeas corpus* and to be released if the detention is not lawful.

Proceedings in Criminal and Penal Matters[5]

11. Any person charged with an offence has the right
    (*a*)   to be informed without unreasonable delay of the specific offence;
    (*b*)   to be tried within a reasonable time;
    (*c*)   not to be compelled to be a witness in proceedings against that person in respect of the offence;
    (*d*)   to be presumed innocent until proven guilty according to law in a fair and public hearing by an independent and impartial tribunal;
    (*e*)   not to be denied reasonable bail without just cause;
    (*f*)   except in the case of an offence under military law tried before a military tribunal, to the benefit of trial by jury where the maximum punishment for the offence is imprisonment for five years or a more severe punishment;

---

[5]   Note section 11(*c*) as one example of the codification of a common law principle — the rule against self-incrimination.

(*g*)   not to be found guilty on account of any act or omission unless, at the time of the act or omission, it constituted an offence under Canadian or international law or was criminal according to the general principles of law recognized by the community of nations;

(*h*)   if finally acquitted of the offence, not to be tried for it again and, if finally found guilty and punished for the offence, not to be tried or punished for it again; and

(*i*)   if found guilty of the offence and if the punishment for the offence has been varied between the time of the commission and the time of sentencing, to the benefit of the lesser punishment.

Treatment or Punishment

12. Everyone has the right not to be subjected to any cruel and unusual treatment or punishment.

Self-incrimination

13. A witness who testifies in any proceedings has the right not to have any incriminating evidence so given used to incriminate that witness in any other proceedings, except in a prosecution for perjury or for the giving of contradictory evidence.

Interpreter

14. A party or witness in any proceedings who does not understand or speak the language in which the proceedings are conducted or who is deaf has the right to the assistance of an interpreter.

HOW THE CHARTER AFFECTS THE SECURITY INDUSTRY

Charter rights impact on the security profession in three main areas:

- *arrest* — the rights of security officers to arrest in the course of their employment;
- *search* — the employer's right to search employees, their lockers, personal effects like lunch buckets and purses and other searches in the workplace and whether evidence seized may be used in a criminal prosecution;
- *confessions* — whether an employee has the right to counsel when being questioned during a company-initiated investigation.

When Security Acts as a "Governmental Function"

When is it permissible for security officers to assume public authority? When criminal activity is in progress, security personnel can assume the authority to search, seize, arrest and detain suspects in the same way that any citizen can assume the public responsibility to avert crime. The additional rights of security officers employed by an enterprise are detailed in Chapter 5, "Criminal Law".

The courts have confirmed a citizen's right to make an arrest describing it as a "governmental function" that must comply with the rights of the arrested person under the *Canadian Charter of Rights and Freedoms*.[6]

In order for evidence such as a confession or a seized exhibit to be admissible at trial, security officers must protect the same Charter rights of the accused as those protected by the police.

There is a fine distinction, depending on the facts, as to whether a person is arrested or detained for some other purpose. In *R. v. Shafie*[7] an accused employee was called into the office of a private investigator hired by the employer. Mr. Justice Krever stated:

> It is apparent from the cases to which I have referred that the weight of judicial opinion, although perhaps not authority in the strict sense, is that actions that, at the hands of the police or other state or government agents, would be a detention, do not amount to a detention within the meaning of s. 10(*b*) of the Charter when done by private or non-governmental persons.

Mr. Justice Beckett in *R. v. A. (J.)*[8] stated:

> I conclude the law to be that any arrest by a private person, which includes a security officer, would trigger the application of the Charter whereas if an accused is merely detained, in a situation that does not amount to an arrest, then the Charter would not apply.

CONCLUSION

From the discussions in this chapter, we have learned that Charter rights in Canada are derived from English common law. The *Canadian Charter of Rights and Freedoms*, which was enacted into federal legislation in 1982 at the time of the repatriation of the Canadian Constitution, legislated these protections to freedom of speech and religious practice and established an obligation on Canada's populace to act in ways that prohibit discriminatory and cruel practices.

The relationship between truth-seeking justice and Charter rights was also examined. The ability of "agents" of enforcement to collect evidence using search warrants and other judicial instruments was noted; *i.e.*, in carrying out their duties of search, investigation, testing, arrest or detention, security people themselves have specific rights, whether working on

---

6   *R. v. Lerke* (1986), 25 D.L.R. (4th) 403, 24 C.C.C. (3d) 129 (Alta. C.A.).
7   (1989), 47 C.C.C. (3d) 27 at 34, 68 C.R. (3d) 259 (Ont. C.A.).
8   [1992] O.J. No. 182 (QL) (Ont. U.F. Ct.), at p. 20.

behalf of an employer or acting as private citizens in assuming "governmental responsibilities" to protect the public against criminal activity. For further analysis of security's role in the protection of privacy and property, in arrest and detention activities, in conducting investigative work and in the gathering of evidence, read on.

4

Privacy Legislation and the Duties of Security to Protect Privacy

INTRODUCTION

Whether hiring new employees or conducting investigations on alleged breaches of conduct by existing employees, businesses deal with personal information every day. How they collect, retain, use and dispose of that information is the subject of this chapter. As you will see in Chapter 7, "Security and Human Resource Law", security departments must be cognizant of the privacy protections afforded to all Canadian citizens as their staffs gather and retain the personal information they believe necessary for proper business administration, for management of internal and external investigations and even for maintaining personal employee information within access control systems. Typically, security departments maintain personal information in secure files or database systems and limit access to authorized users on a need-to-know basis. Security also plays a role in assisting other departments within the organization to properly secure personal information.

Generally speaking, personal data retained in an organization's database about each employee and considered sensitive includes:

- age, name, ID numbers, income, ethnic origin, blood type;
- opinions, evaluations, comments, social status, disciplinary actions; and
- employee files, credit records, loan records, medical records, existence of a dispute between a consumer and merchant, intentions (*e.g.*, acquire goods, change jobs).

In most cases, confidential information is not released, except in the following circumstances:

- where the person to whom the information relates has identified that information and has consented to its disclosure;

- to an officer or employee of the business in which the employee works who needs the information in the performance of his or her duty;
- to a federal or provincial governmental authority;
- to an institution or law enforcement agency in Canada to aid in an investigation undertaken because of a law enforcement proceeding or from which a law enforcement proceeding may result;
- where disclosure is necessary to aid in the investigation of allegations that individuals have made false statements or engaged in other misleading conduct at work;
- in compassionate circumstances, to facilitate contact with the next of kin or a friend of an individual who is ill, injured or deceased; or
- to a person who has been authorized by the employee to whom the information relates to make an inquiry on that employee's behalf, or to a person whom an employee has identified as next of kin or legal representative if the employee is incapacitated.

When in doubt about the type of information that can be released, security people should consult with human resources, legal counsel or the manager who has been designated as responsible for privacy matters.

Security professionals must work within the Canadian legal system with respect to the collection, use, retention and disposal of confidential and/or personal information.

THE FEDERAL STATUTE

Canada's *Personal Information Protection and Electronic Documents Act*[1] (*"PIPEDA"*) was created as a result of a directive issued by the European Union requiring that any country wishing to engage in business with the European Union establish regulations regarding the gathering and protection of personal information. It also required that "fair business practices" be implemented. The purpose of *PIPEDA*, as stated in section 3, is to:

> . . . establish, in an era in which technology increasingly facilitates the circulation and exchange of information, rules to govern the collection, use and disclosure of personal information in a manner that recognizes the right of privacy of individuals with respect to their personal information and the need of organizations to collect, use or disclose personal information for purposes that a reasonable person would consider appropriate in the circumstances.

---

[1]   S.C. 2000, c. 5.

The Act was designed to regulate the manner in which businesses and other private organizations collect, use and disclose personal information in the course of commercial activities and to ensure that the overarching principle of reasonableness is applied to information practices in the private sector.

Until *PIPEDA* came into effect in 2001, only information held by government organizations was subject to legislation regarding access to information or privacy. No such legislative protection was afforded to information held by private businesses. *PIPEDA* attempts to address the absence of protection in the private sector by setting a standard to be followed for federally regulated businesses, interprovincial and international flow of information, and requiring the provinces to enact similar protections for provincially regulated businesses.

Once it took effect, the Act applied to:

- all organizations engaged in federal works, undertakings or businesses;
- information being disclosed or shared for profit across a national or provincial border; and
- all organizations engaged in commercial activities in any of the three jurisdictions (federal, provincial and territorial).

As of January 1, 2002, the Act was extended to cover personal health information in the possession of any of these organizations, and beginning January 1, 2004, the Act expanded to cover information collected in the course of all commercial activity within a province, as well as in provincially regulated industries.[2] Importantly, however, if a province enacts legislation substantially similar to *PIPEDA*, that provincial legislation will exclusively apply to information collected in the course of commercial activity within the province, as well as to provincially regulated industries.[3]

---

[2] Section 30(1) and (1.1). The purpose and phasing-in process is discussed in a publication put out by the Office of the Privacy Commissioner of Canada entitled *Your Privacy Rights: Canada's Personal Information Protection and Electronic Documents Act* (February, 2001).

[3] On November 19, 2003, Quebec's private sector legislation (*An Act respecting the Protection of Personal Information in the Private Sector*, R.S.Q., c. P-39.1) was officially recognized as substantially similar. Organizations in Quebec will not be subject to *PIPEDA* and will instead continue to be subject to the Quebec private sector privacy law that also provides Quebecers with a general right of access to and correction of personal information.

Does PIPEDA Apply to My Organization?

The Act applies in two ways to personal information held by an organization. First, it applies generally to all information collected by an organization in the course of commercial activities. In clarifying the relevant terms, section 2 of *PIPEDA* defines "organization" as including "an association, a partnership, a person and a trade union". It also defines "commercial activities" as "any particular transaction, act or conduct or any regular course of conduct that is of a commercial character, including the selling, bartering or leasing of donor, membership or other fundraising lists". It should finally be noted that the term "personal information" refers to "information about an identifiable individual, but does not include the name, title or business address or telephone number of an employee of an organization". There is also some argument that the Act may apply to information about a small company that is essentially a one-person organization.

Second, the Act applies to information collected about an employee of an organization if that organization is a "federal work, undertaking or business". That definition in section 2 of the Act contains an inclusive list of examples, including airports and airlines, banks, telecommunications companies, and any work, undertaking or business that is not under the exclusive jurisdiction of a provincial legislature. Whether your organization is subject to provincial or federal jurisdiction can be a complicated issue and one that is best left to your organization's legal counsel to determine. In some cases, an activity can be both federal and provincial. For example, workers in an oilfield may be under provincial jurisdiction while working on a provincial pipeline, but under federal jurisdiction while working on an interprovincial pipeline. Employee information held by organizations that are not federal works, undertakings or businesses and are *not* currently nor ever expected to be covered by the Act falls under the exclusive jurisdiction of the provinces.[4]

Collection and Use

Schedule 1 to *PIPEDA* sets out the general principles and guidelines that constitute the National Standard of Canada (Canadian Standards Association's) *Model Code for the Protection of Personal Information*.[5] The Code sets out the principles that must be followed by organizations in order to protect personal information.

---

[4]   S. Perrin, H.H. Black, D.H. Flaherty and T.M. Rankin, *The Personal Information Protection and Electronic Documents Act: An Annotated Guide* (Concord, Ont.: Irwin Law, 2001), Chapter 6, or see the Quicklaw Database: PIPE.

[5]   CAN/CSA-Q830-96.

Consent

Organizations are required to develop policies and procedures that implement the Code's principles. For example, organizations need to communicate through their policies and procedures the requirement to obtain consent from individuals, including employees, to collect, use and disclose personal information (clause 4.3). They must also retain evidence that the consent was obtained and that the information was gathered for the purposes identified. This is not to imply that consent is necessary in all cases; however, if consent is possible, it ought to be obtained prior to collection. The Act recognizes that obtaining consent is not always possible nor always desirable. Specific circumstances under which information may be collected without the consent of the individual are:

- when the collection is clearly in the interests of the individual and the information cannot be obtained in another manner — for instance, a person collapses in a private medical clinic and, in order to treat him, the nurse must access his medical history through a database without his consent since he cannot provide the information himself;
- where it is reasonably foreseeable that obtaining consent would impact the accuracy or availability of the information being sought, specifically with regard to breach of provincial or federal law or a private agreement (an example of this might be an employee suspected of stealing from his or her employer, who cannot be expected to provide accurate information regarding the matter — in this case, the employee is in breach of his or her employment contract, justifying the investigator's collection of personal information from a source other than the employee or without the employee's consent);
- for journalistic and artistic purposes and information that is publicly available.

Schedule 1 to *PIPEDA* lists several examples of how to obtain consent for the collection of information, such as by means of a consent form. While the Code does recognize "implied" consent, it is best to obtain "express" consent (clause 4.3.6).

Limiting Collection

In all cases, however, there is an obligation to limit the collection of personal information (clause 4.4), whether consented to or not, to the minimum required to fulfil the purpose specified. In addition, information ought only to be maintained for as long as is necessary to fulfil the stated purpose. For example, the personal information submitted by an individual to a bank for the purposes of securing a loan must be purged from the bank's data records once the application has been considered. If an alternate purpose for using the information arises, consent should be sought again for the new purpose. And, to repeat, if it is not practical to gain consent (where it would affect the accuracy or even the acquisition of the information) and the information is being collected in the investigation of a breach of an agreement or law, then consent does not need to be obtained.

Accuracy

The Code emphasizes the need for accuracy in the collection of personal information (clause 4.6). The goal is to ensure that only correct information based on truth is used to make decisions about individuals — this provision is clearly very significant for the investigation and security industries. The general obligation here raises two specific concerns: protecting the information from outside influence and unauthorized access by ensuring that it is securely maintained; and allowing individuals the right to access and correct mistakes in their personal information.

Individual Access

The right to access one's personal information that is held by an organization is guaranteed by the Code (clause 4.9). However, if an individual under investigation by a security company were to request access to his or her personal information, the security company involved would not simply open up its file room; rather, it would direct the person to the officer within the organization who has been delegated the responsibility for maintaining compliance with the Act.

There is one exception to an individual's right to access his or her own information — that is when the information was collected without the individual's consent pursuant to an investigation of the breach of an agreement or a law. However, if access is denied for this reason, the organization must notify the Privacy Commissioner of Canada and explain why access is not being granted. The end result is that the individual will likely be allowed access to his or her own personal information. It is therefore imperative that investigators restrict the information they collect to that which is necessary for the purpose, ensure its accuracy and do not include personal opinions or commentary about irrelevant issues (such as an individual's character). Under clause 4.9.5 the individual has the right to request that his or her personal information be corrected and, if inaccuracy or incompleteness is demonstrated, the organization is obligated to amend the information. An unsuccessful challenge to the information's accuracy must also be noted on the information record. It is, once again, best to forward such a request to the company official responsible for ensuring compliance, who may be well advised to obtain legal advice on more complicated matters.

Disclosure

The consent principle (clause 4.3) also applies to disclosure of personal information. This principle obligates an organization to prevent the disclosure of personal information in its care or control. One aspect of this obligation is to take security measures that are appropriate to the level of sensitivity of the information, as required by clause 4.7. This includes: physical measures, such as locked cabinets and restricted access to offices; organizational measures, such as security clearances and the limiting of disclosure and use of information to a "need-to-know" basis; and technological measures, such as the use of passwords and encryption.

Section 7(3) of *PIPEDA* elaborates on clause 4.3 and limits it in some respects. Clause 4.3 contains a very broad statement of principle — that any disclosure must be consensual. However, the principle does allow for disclosure without consent in matters relating to law enforcement, where notifying the individual would defeat the purpose of collection. Parliament decided that this was far too broad an exception to the general rule of consent and has limited it significantly by section 7(3), which states:

> 7(3) For the purpose of clause 4.3 of Schedule 1, and *despite the note that accompanies that clause*, an organization may disclose personal information without the knowledge or consent of the individual only if . . .

(Emphasis added.) Section 7(3) then goes on to list a number of situations where such disclosure is permitted, including disclosure:

- to a barrister or solicitor who is representing the organization (section 7(3)(*a*));
- for the purpose of collecting a debt owed by the individual to the organization (section 7(3)(*b*));
- to comply with a subpoena, warrant, court order, or the court's rules (section 7(3)(*c*));
- to a government institution that has requested the information with lawful authority, with respect to national security, defence, international affairs, law enforcement, or the administration of laws (section 7(3)(*c.*1));
- to an investigative body or government institution, when the organization has reasonable grounds to believe that the information relates to a breach of an agreement or law, or relates to national security, defence or international affairs (section 7(3)(*d*));
- to a person who needs the information during an emergency that threatens the individual in question and the individual is informed promptly of the disclosure after the fact (section 7(3)(*e*));

- to information that is publicly available and specified in the regulations made under the Act (section 7(3)(*h*.1)); or
- by an investigative body, when reasonable for the investigation of a breach of an agreement or law (section 7(3)(*h*.2)).

For example, external investigators are hired by a company to conduct a fraud investigation on one of its employees. The investigators manage to gather evidence of the fraud and decide that the local police ought to be involved. This disclosure (to the police) would be acceptable under section 7(3)(*d*)(i) because it would be made, on the initiative of the organization, to an investigative body or government institution, and the organization has reason to believe that there has been a breach of a law and/or an agreement. At a later date, these investigators would be required to provide their notes and reports under subpoena or warrant, issued by a judicial or quasi-judicial body. This disclosure would also be acceptable, under section 7(3)(*c*).

What right does a company have to disclose private information to an outside investigative agency? The Privacy Commissioner has expressed the opinion that the investigative company is acting in the capacity of agent for the employer and therefore is eligible to receive the information.

In addition, section 7(3)(*c*.1) allows an organization to release information if it is requested by a government institution that has some lawful authority to obtain it and the information relates to law enforcement or national defence. Consequently, in the case of a terrorist investigation, if the Canadian Security Intelligence Service approached a security firm or in-house security officers requesting access to files that the firm holds on an employee reasonably believed to be involved in terrorist activity, under section 7(3)(*c*.1)(i) disclosure without consent would be appropriate.

Notes on "Investigative Bodies"

Investigative bodies are mentioned twice in *PIPEDA*, granting them broader authority to disclose personal information, or have it disclosed to them. The first instance is in section 7(3)(*d*), which allows organizations to disclose information to "an investigative body, a government institution or a part of a government institution and the organization" when it is believed that the information relates to a breach of the law or an issue of national security. The second place where this term is used is in section 7(3)(*h*.2), which allows investigative bodies to disclose information for the purposes of investigating a breach of a law or an agreement.

Two investigative bodies have been granted status by regulation:[6] the Insurance Crime Prevention Bureau, a division of the Insurance Council

---

[6]   *Regulations Specifying Investigative Bodies*, SOR/2001-6.

of Canada; and the Bank Crime Prevention and Investigation Office of the Canadian Bankers' Association. Private investigators as a class are not identified but the Privacy Commissioner has issued an opinion that they will not receive an exemption. All applications for designation as an investigative body are reviewed by Industry Canada, which has set up several criteria regarding necessary qualifications. Applications are considered on a case-by-case basis.[7]

Monitoring Employee Communications

Employee monitoring, involving telephone, e-mail, Internet use and video surveillance, is permissible in Canada, provided that the motive for the monitoring is reasonable and employees have been forewarned. The monitoring policy may be outlined as a condition of employment in the original employment contract that employees are required to sign before they begin work at a company's facility. As has already been discussed, employers have an obligation to provide a work environment that is free of discrimination and harassment and in which employee privacy rights under the *Criminal Code*[8] are safeguarded while, at the same time, protecting confidential business information. The test seems to be one of determining whether an employer's monitoring activities violate the reasonable expectation on the part of an employee that no person other than the intended recipient would have an opportunity to intercept his or her messages. For this reason it is important that policies regarding a company's e-mail and business network usage are spelled out and that information systems are protected by passwords and other technological barriers to unauthorized use. Advice from counsel should be sought before acting on information obtained from any interception of employee e-mail. Chapter 8, "Evidence", deals with the legal issues of video surveillance.

THE PROVINCIAL STATUTES

PIPEDA requires that each province implement substantially similar legislation, failing which the federal statute will apply within the province. Security professionals should be familiar with any provincial privacy legislation enacted in their jurisdiction.

---

[7] See Perrin et al., *op. cit.*, footnote 4.
[8] R.S.C. 1985, c. C-46.

Freedom of Information and Protection of Privacy Acts

Most of the provinces, as well as the federal government, have passed freedom of information and protection of privacy Acts of some description. These Acts serve two main purposes:

* to establish a right of access to information held by a government organization; and
* to protect the privacy of individuals by limiting the means by which government organizations are able to collect, maintain, use and disclose personal information.

The federal government has both an *Access to Information Act*[9] and a *Privacy Act*.[10] Some provinces have also passed privacy Acts that create a tort of breach of privacy. Our concern here is the privacy side of such pieces of legislation.

Collection

As stated above, these statutes are generally designed to limit the collection, maintenance, use and disclosure of personal information. The Acts generally limit collection in two ways:

1. They limit the type of information to be gathered by specifically listing the instances when personal information may be collected. The relevant sections are often set out in checklist format, listing instances such as investigation into a breach of the law, or determination of eligibility for an award or benefit.
2. They limit how the information may be collected, such as requiring that personal information be collected directly from the individual, except in specifically prescribed circumstances. Here again, organizations investigating breaches of law are often exempted from this requirement.

Personal information, therefore, should only be collected as prescribed under the appropriate section of the relevant freedom of information or privacy Act and it must be collected directly from the individual, unless the Act specifically allows for circumstances that bypass the need for consent.

Accuracy, Protection and Correction

Freedom of information and protection of privacy Acts, much like *PIPEDA*, usually contain provisions requiring that a public body ensure the information collected is accurate. One of the ways this is achieved is

---

[9]   R.S.C. 1985, c. A-1.
[10]   R.S.C. 1985, c. P-21.

by giving the individual who is the subject of the collected data access to what has been recorded and, if it can be shown that the information is incorrect, by providing him or her with an opportunity to have it be corrected. This, at times, can be problematic in that individuals will often disagree with non-factual items in a report, such as opinions or inferences, and request a correction. The Acts do not generally require such corrections; however, some Acts, such as the British Columbia legislation,[11] do require the public body to add a notation to the disputed information explaining that the applicant disagrees with the information in the file. For this reason, it is important to record only factual, complete and accurate information, rather than opinion (unless required to do so). Finally, the public body has an obligation to protect all duly obtained personal information from inappropriate collection, use, disclosure or destruction by adopting any reasonable security measures within its power.

Use and Disclosure

Freedom of information and privacy Acts also limit the use, disclosure and destruction aspects of any collected information. Generally speaking, the information may only be used or disclosed for the purpose for which it was collected, unless the individual has consented to a new use, or unless the new use is consistent in purpose with the old use. Several Acts contain "consistent purpose" definitions and provide additional detail on what is considered to be a purpose consistent with the original. Once again, the Acts usually set out a long list of specific instances where alternate uses may be made of information, often citing the prevention or investigation of a breach of law.

Privacy Impact Assessments

Specific to each Act, there are tools available regarding the collection, use and disclosure of personal information. The department given the mandate of enforcing and governing a particular freedom of information or privacy Act creates most of these tools. They are often presented in the form of a checklist or decision matrix. An excellent example is the Privacy Impact Assessment Tool, which can be found on the British Columbia Information and Privacy Commissioner's website.[12] While this tool is specific to the British Columbia statute, it contains many similarities to other jurisdictions.

---

[11] *Freedom of Information and Protection of Privacy Act*, R.S.B.C. 1996, c. 165, s. 29.
[12] Available at www.oipcbc.org/public/pia.

Proactive Strategies

The following are some proactive strategies and best practices for gathering and handling personal information:

- If you do not *need* the information for a specific reason or program, do not collect it.
- If it does not appear that you have specific *authority* to collect or disclose information, do not collect or disclose it. Find out who is in authority and pass the request on to them.
- *Be aware* of who is around you when you discuss specific cases with your work colleagues.
- When talking over cases with colleagues from other companies or corporations, *generalize* the information by removing personal identifiers that would point to the individual being discussed (*e.g.*, name, occupation, etc.).
- Should you receive any requests for access to personal information in your possession, it is best to *first determine*:
  - whether provincial or federal statutes apply in the situation;
  - whether specific company policies and procedures apply;
  - whether anyone has been designated responsible for privacy compliance within the organization and whether the requests for access should be forwarded to that designated individual.[13]

CONCLUSION

Good privacy practices extend beyond the legislative requirements laid out in the federal and provincial statutes. They begin with ethical considerations about how to deal with sensitive, personal information. They are integrated into every aspect of business. They involve generalizing information when discussing cases with colleagues so that an individual cannot be identified, either directly or through inference. They also involve routine practices, such as keeping offices locked and putting away papers containing personal information when not in use. The ethics of information management must be clearly understood by all members of an organization. For this reason, concise and clearly communicated privacy policies should be a priority.

---

[13] See section 9 of *PIPEDA*.

5
Criminal Law

INTRODUCTION

Without an in-depth understanding of Canadian criminal law, it is impossible to administer a security program. Organizations rely on security professionals because they have a thorough knowledge of the criminal justice system and are competent to co-ordinate investigations with law enforcement. In fact, investigations by a company's security department often parallel those undertaken by law enforcement. Consequently, they must be conducted properly; otherwise, the organization might not be in a position to prosecute and could be involved in civil litigation as a result of investigative improprieties.

The following situation illustrates the complexity of a security investigation:

> *A disgruntled employee, on the verge of being dismissed, sets fire to a building on the work site. The fire results in the death of two employees who were in the building and — as a result of the fire and the subsequent investigation of the arson and deaths — the company's operations are shut down for several days. Because of the criminal actions of the employee, the company terminates his employment and the police initiate an investigation for arson, murder and manslaughter. The following court actions result:*
>
> 1. *The company sues the employee for damages as a result of lost profits from the plant shutdown.*
> 2. *The employee is terminated and the union gives notice of arbitration of the dismissal.*
> 3. *Because of the fatalities, the families of the deceased employees sue the ex-employee. They also sue the company for failure to provide proper security for the family members who were killed.*
> 4. *The police charge the ex-employee with arson and manslaughter.*

> 5. *The Workers' Compensation Board gives notice to the company that an assessment will be levied as a result of the deaths of the employees.*

What if the prosecutor decides to stay proceedings on the criminal charges against the former employee because there is insufficient evidence to proceed with criminal charges or because no witness is available?

What effect will this have on the position of the company in arbitration proceedings or civil actions?

What effect will this have on the civil actions by the families against the company or the former employee?

ELEMENTS OF A CRIMINAL ACT

There are two ingredients to a criminal act: the *actus reus*; and the *mens rea*. It has often been said that "the intent and the act must both concur to constitute the crime".

Actus Reus

The *actus reus* includes all of the overt acts performed by the accused that constitute the commission of the offence (the "guilty act"). Hence, a witness who observed the crime or any part of it in progress can provide testimony about his or her observations.

Mens Rea

The *mens rea* is the intent of the accused to commit the offence. Difficult to measure, *mens rea* amounts to the attempt to recreate and describe what was going on in the mind of the accused (*viz.,* the "guilty mind"). Because it is obviously impossible to know with any degree of certainty the thought processes and state of mind of an accused, a judge or jury ruling on a case must infer from all of the other surrounding facts whether or not the accused intended to commit the offence.

ABSOLUTE AND STRICT LIABILITY OFFENCES

Not all federal, provincial or *Criminal Code* offences require *mens rea*. Over the years, the courts have developed the principles of absolute and strict liability to apply to numerous offences. In the case of absolute liability, criminal responsibility is established irrespective of fault and the Crown Prosecutor need only prove the *actus reus*; the *mens rea* follows naturally. In the case of strict liability, simple negligence is determined. Although extremely complex, these legal principles allow judges to rule fairly in cases where an individual is convicted of an offence such as criminal negligence causing death. By way of example, the principles of absolute and strict liability can be used to repudiate the defence raised in a drunk-driver case, that impairment from alcohol prevented the driver from forming the intent to commit the offence.

Several sections in the *Criminal Code* demonstrate this departure from the requirement to show *mens rea*. In such cases, language such as "ought to", "reasonable care", "good reason", "reasonable grounds" and "reasonably expected" is employed. Offences of this nature are most commonly associated with contraventions of provincial and federal statutes. For example, the highway traffic Acts of many provinces allow the police to charge the owner of a vehicle with speeding simply by establishing that the automobile exceeded the speed limit (usually by means of a camera-radar system). There is no need to prove that the owner was driving the car at the time or that the driver had any knowledge of having exceeded the speed limit.

SUMMARY CONVICTION AND INDICTABLE OFFENCES

Criminal activities are either summary conviction or indictable offences, although some offences in the *Criminal Code* may be dual procedure or "hybrid".

Summary Conviction Offences

Summary conviction offences are those considered by the legislators to be "less serious" offences. Their counterparts in the United States are known as "misdemeanors". They are governed by provincial summary conviction Acts that incorporate Part XXVII of the *Criminal Code* and are tried by the lower courts as offences against such provincial statutes as highway traffic and liquor Acts. A summary judgment is a procedural device intended to promote prompt disposition without a formal trial of minor cases where the facts are not in dispute or only a question of law is involved.

EXAMPLES OF SUMMARY CONVICTION OFFENCES	
Criminal Offence	Slang Terminology
indecent act	indecent exposure
disturbing the peace	
prowling at night	peeping Tom

Indictable Offences

Indictable offences are more serious infractions of the law and require prosecution by a government authority. In the United States, these are known as "felonies".

There are three types of indictable offences:

1. Those that must be heard in a lower court by a Provincial Court Judge.[1] These include theft, acting under false pretences, fraud and mischief.

2. Those in which the accused has the right to elect whether the case is heard in a lower or higher court. If the higher court is elected, there may be a preliminary hearing in the lower court to decide if there is enough evidence for the accused to stand trial.[2] This type includes all offences not covered by type 1 above or type 3 below.

3. Those that must be heard by a higher court or by a judge and jury. These offences include treason, alarming Her Majesty, mutiny, piracy, murder and the attempted bribery of a holder of judicial office.[3]

---

[1] Section 553 of the *Criminal Code* lists these offences.
[2] Sections 554 and 555 of the *Criminal Code*.
[3] Section 469 of the *Criminal Code* lists these offences.

EXAMPLES OF INDICTABLE OFFENCES	
Criminal Offence	Slang Terminology
theft or possession of property obtained by crime (where the value exceeds $5000)	pilferage
breaking and entering	burglary
fraud (over $5000)	larceny
false pretences (over $5000)	kiting
robbery	mugging
aggravated sexual assault	rape
arson	torching
secret commissions	bribery, kickbacks

Dual Procedure Offences

In dual procedure offences, the Crown Prosecutor may elect to proceed either by way of summary conviction or by way of indictment. In making a decision, the prosecutor will consider the seriousness of the alleged facts surrounding the case and the previous convictions of the accused. In a case of assault causing bodily harm where there were only minor injuries to the victim and no previous convictions on the record of the accused, the prosecutor may decide to proceed by way of summary conviction. However, if the victim was badly injured and the accused has a long history of assaults, the prosecutor will usually elect to proceed by indictment.

The following chart identifies offences deemed to be indictable until the prosecutor elects how to proceed.[4]

---

4 Section 34 of the *Interpretation Act*, R.S.C. 1985, c. I-21.

EXAMPLES OF DUAL PROCEDURE OFFENCES	
Criminal Offence	Slang Terminology
theft or possession of property obtained by crime (where value is under $5000)	pilferage or petty theft
mischief	wilful damage
mischief in relation to computer data	hacking
unauthorized use of a computer	hacking
obstructing a peace officer	
assault	battery
assault with intent to resist arrest	resisting arrest
fraud (under $5000)	petty larceny
false pretences (under $5000)	kiting
sexual assault (that is not aggravated sexual assault)	molestation

RIGHTS OF ARREST ALLOWED THE SECURITY PRACTITIONER

In effecting an arrest, a police officer, private citizen or security officer is depriving another individual of his or her freedom. It is no surprise that the whole area of arrest is extremely complex and subject to scrutiny. It is an area of the law that the security officer must thoroughly understand.

The security professional has three powers of arrest all of which are described in the *Criminal Code*:[5]

---

[5]   Sections 494 and 31.

- the citizen's power of arrest;
- the power of arrest of a property owner or person authorized by the owner; and
- the power of arrest for breach of the peace.

What Constitutes an Arrest?

Whether an arrest has been properly effected may be important for two reasons:

1. If the person being arrested resists, a charge of resisting arrest may be laid, but the Crown must be in a position to establish that the arrest was lawful in the first place.[6]
2. If there is a civil action for false arrest, the plaintiff must be able to prove that an arrest occurred that caused a loss of liberty.

The courts have held that for an arrest to be completed handcuffs need not be used, nor is the laying of hands on the individual necessary. A restraint "by an assertion of authority" or words used to show a sense of compulsion may be sufficient if the person submits or acquiesces in the deprivation of liberty. Under the right circumstances, the words "Come with me" may suffice.

Mr. Justice Roger Salhany adopted Justice Roy Moreland's definition of "arrest" in his authoritative text:[7]

> "Mere words, however, do not constitute an arrest. There must be some actual restraint of the person of the arrestee or he must submit in a situation where the officer has the power of control. So to merely say to the accused that he is under arrest is not enough unless he submits and the officer is in a position to effect a seizure if desired."

and noted Sir Patrick Devlin's comment on Moreland:

> "Arrest and imprisonment are in law the same thing. Any form of physical restraint is an arrest and imprisonment is only a continuing arrest."[8]

---

[6] See *R. v. Orban* (1972), 8 C.C.C. (2d) 518, 20 C.R. (N.S.) 46 (Sask. Q.B.), where a store security officer arrested the accused for shoplifting and they were charged with resisting arrest. The accused were acquitted of the theft charges at trial and the Court of Queen's Bench overturned their convictions for common assault on the security officer on the grounds that it was not a legal arrest because she did not "see them committing an indictable offence".

[7] R. Salhany, *Canadian Criminal Procedure*, 5th ed. (Aurora, Ont.: Canada Law Book, 1989), at p. 39, quoting from R. Moreland, *Modern Criminal Procedure* (New York: Bobbs-Merrill, 1959).

[8] Salhany, *ibid.*, at p. 39, quoting from P. Devlin, *The Criminal Prosecution in England* (New Haven, Conn.: Yale, 1958).

Any legal consideration concerning whether an arrest has taken place will be based on the facts pertaining to the circumstances of the arrest.[9]

Why Arrest?

Under *most* circumstances, an arrest will not be necessary in security situations or security investigations. However, a security officer may be put in a position where an arrest is necessary:

- to identify the accused;
- to recover stolen property or protect evidence that may be in the possession of the accused; or
- where the accused person is drunk, violent or suicidal — to protect that person or others.

Citizen's Power of Arrest

The first consideration of the power of a security officer to arrest is whether such a power exists for any citizen. In other words, can the security officer in the course of his or her duties simply use the power of the citizen? The obvious answer is "yes".

The right and duty of a citizen to effect an arrest were established at common law in early England. At a time when there were no police officers but it was necessary to protect the prerogative of the King's peace, every citizen was given the right to arrest individuals without warrant for the more serious offences. The common law right was codified in Canada's *Criminal Code* in section 494(1) and provides that anyone may arrest without warrant:

(*a*)   a person whom he finds committing an indictable offence;[10] or
(*b*)   a person who, on reasonable and probable grounds, he believes
   (i)   has committed a criminal offence, and
   (ii)   is escaping from and freshly pursued by persons who have lawful authority to arrest that person.

It is important to note that the offence must be indictable. The section is therefore not helpful to the average citizen who must determine before the arrest is attempted whether a summary conviction or an indictable offence was committed. The second portion of the section allows a private citizen to assist in an arrest where law enforcement is in fresh pursuit of an accused. In order to establish fresh pursuit, continuous pursuit must be evident with proof of reasonable diligence by the pursuing officer.

---

[9]   *R. v. Whitfield* (1969), 7 D.L.R. (3d) 97, [1970] 1 C.C.C. 129 (S.C.C.).
[10]   Remember that a dual procedure offence is assumed to be indictable until the prosecutor elects how to proceed.

One authority on criminal law states:[11]

> Where a private citizen chooses to arrest without a warrant, he runs the risk that if the person arrested is innocent and the arrest therefore wrongful, he will be held liable for damages for false imprisonment. He is, however, entitled to set up the defence that he believed on reasonable and probable grounds that the accused had committed a criminal offence . . .

Reasonable and probable grounds are more than mere suspicion. Observation is key: the perpetrator must be "seen in the act".

Effect of the Charter of Rights on Arrest

As was discussed in Chapter 3, "The Canadian Charter of Rights and Freedoms", the courts have confirmed the citizen's right to make an arrest and have described it as a "governmental function" that must comply with the rights of the arrested person, as established under the *Canadian Charter of Rights and Freedoms*.[12] Section 10 of the Charter provides in part:

- Everyone has the right, on arrest, to be informed of the reasons for the arrest.
- Everyone has the right, on arrest, to retain and instruct counsel without delay and to be informed of that right.
- Everyone has the right to have the validity of the detention tested legally and to be released if the detention is not lawful (the common law right of *habeas corpus*).

In order for evidence such as a confession or a seized exhibit to be admissible at trial, security officers must follow the same procedures used by the police in reading Charter rights to an accused at the time of arrest.

Arrest by Property Owner or Person Authorized

The second (and more useful) power of arrest that can be used by the security professional is found in section 494(2) of the *Criminal Code*:

> 494(2) Any one who is
> (*a*) the owner or a person in lawful possession of property, or
> (*b*) a person authorized by the owner or a by a person in lawful possession of property,
> may arrest without warrant a person whom he finds committing a criminal offence on or in relation to that property.

Section 494(2) gives much broader power to the security officer in two respects:

---

[11] Salhany, *op. cit.*, footnote 7, at p. 45.
[12] *R. v. Lerke* (1986), 25 D.L.R. (4th) 403, 24 C.C.C. (3d) 129 (Alta. C.A.).

1. Section 494(2) applies to all "criminal" offences, not just indictable offences mentioned in section 494(1).
2. There are four classes of individuals who may arrest:
   * the owner of the property;
   * other individuals in lawful possession, *e.g.*, a lessee;
   * a person authorized by the owner, *e.g.*, a security officer;
   * a person authorized by the individual in lawful possession, *e.g.*, a security officer or security company hired by the lessee or property manager to protect the property.

The section also contemplates three classes of offences:

   * an offence committed on the premises against the property of the owner or person in lawful possession, *e.g.*, theft of material from a facility;
   * an offence committed on the property against the person or property of someone else, *e.g.*, a sexual attack against an employee or the theft of another person's tools;
   * an offence committed off the premises but directed at the facility, *e.g.*, someone throws a rock through a window.

Note, however, that section 494(2) maintains the "finds committing" requirement found in subsection (1). Where the security officer did not observe the offence being committed, he or she does not have the power to arrest.

> *A worker observes someone stealing tools from a maintenance shop and placing them in a personal vehicle. The worker reports the matter to security and the vehicle is stopped at the front gate, the tools are seized and the driver is arrested.*
>
> *Question: Did security have authority to arrest the suspect?*
>
> *Answer: Security, if they proceed under the powers of arrest granted by section 494(1), did not see the theft being committed and would therefore not have the power to arrest the accused for theft. It may still be a legal arrest, however, because at the time the suspect approached the gate he was committing the offence of possession of stolen property and security did find him committing that offence.*

Arrest for Breach of the Peace

The third power of arrest is found in section 30 of the *Criminal Code*:

> 30. Every one who witnesses a breach of the peace is justified in interfering to prevent the continuance or renewal thereof and may detain any

person who commits or is about to join in or to renew the breach of the peace, for the purpose of giving him into the custody of a peace officer, if he uses no more force than is reasonably necessary to prevent the continuance or renewal of the breach of the peace or than is reasonably proportioned to the danger to be apprehended from the continuance or renewal of the breach of the peace.

The detention power covered here is a power of arrest that a security officer may use where someone is causing a disturbance by:[13]

- fighting;
- screaming;
- shouting;
- swearing;
- singing;
- using insulting or obscene language;
- being drunk;
- impeding or molesting others;
- loitering and obstructing others.

The court will consider the extent of the interruption "such as the causing of some disorder or agitation or interference with the ordinary and customary use by the public or a public place".[14]

Duties After an Arrest

There are four duties that must be carried out after an arrest and security officers should perform them or risk the possibility of a civil action:

Call the Police

The *Criminal Code* provides:

> 494(3) Any one other than a peace office who arrests a person without a warrant shall forthwith deliver the person to a peace officer.

Note that section 30 cited earlier states "for the purpose of giving him into the custody of a peace officer". In section 494 the word "forthwith" does not mean that the arrested person must be taken directly to a police officer, but that the person arresting must do what is reasonable and practical under the circumstances. In most cases, this means that the police will be called to attend and pick up the prisoner.

An interesting issue was raised at a 1995 conference of the Canadian Association of Chiefs of Police regarding police protocol for shoplifting.[15]

---

[13] See section 175(1) of the *Criminal Code*.

[14] *R. v. Wolgram* (1975), 29 C.C.C. (2d) 536 (B.C.S.C.).

[15] *Partnerships, Shoptheft Protocol* (Canadian Association of Chiefs of Police, November, 1995), is now followed in many jurisdictions.

In that protocol it is suggested that security should establish a procedure with the local police force where they would arrest a suspect, obtain identification and call the local police. If there are no outstanding warrants, the suspect could then be released and could be summoned later by the police. In the meantime, the police would be available to respond to more pressing emergency calls and both security and the accused would not have to sit and wait for the police to respond. The implementation of such a protocol raised the question, however, of whether security has the right after an arrest to release the prisoner or whether there is an obligation to turn the apprehended individual over to the police. After some study it was decided that releasing the prisoner, while not specifically following the instructions in section 494, is not, in fact, illegal. The early release serves to protect against a violation of section 9 of the Charter and, because the suspect does not suffer any damages as a result of being released, there is no liability with respect to the restraint.

Notify the Prisoner of the Reason for the Arrest

The Charter requires that persons arrested be made aware of the reasons for the arrest (unless it is impossible because they are putting up a fight, attempting to run away, etc.). It is not necessary that the arresting officer use technical language or refer to specific sections in the *Criminal Code* and, in fact, it is preferable not to do so. Words such as "You are under arrest for stealing this computer" are sufficient. If the officer attempts to quote a section in the *Criminal Code* and uses the wrong section or if the police or prosecutor later decide that charges should be laid under a different section, the arrest may become invalid.

Advise the Person of the Right to Counsel

The Charter also provides that the prisoner has the right to be advised of the right to call a lawyer. The prisoner must be given the opportunity to carry on a private conversation with the lawyer, subject to the officer being able to maintain proper custody and control.

Protect the Person Until the Police Arrive

The arresting officer has a duty to protect the prisoner from harm because the individual is in the officer's custody. Where the person is suicidal or under the influence of drugs or alcohol it may be necessary to use restraint in order to provide protection.[16]

---

[16] See *Lipcsei v. Central Saanich (District)*, [1994] 7 W.W.R. 582, 8 B.C.L.R. (3d) 325 (S.C.), for an example of a case where the police were held liable for 30% of the awarded damages for failing to get medical attention for a prisoner.

How Much Force is Allowed?

One of the most difficult questions in the area of arrest is:"How much force is appropriate to effect the arrest, restrain the arrested person afterwards or stop them from escaping?" Obviously, the reasonableness of the force used will depend on all of the circumstances surrounding the incident.

The officer may use "only as much force as is necessary". If force is necessary, the person making the arrest should use only a restraining force. Once an inappropriately high level of force is used (such as an attempt to incapacitate the prisoner), then there is a stronger likelihood that the person arresting is overstepping what may be considered reasonable force.

In an unreported case, a store security officer arrested a shoplifter. The security officer instructed another store employee to follow the shoplifter's wife into the parking lot and take down the licence number of their vehicle. Instead, the employee attempted to arrest the shoplifter's wife by holding her. He was subsequently charged with assault. The court held that the store employee did not have authority to arrest the shoplifter's wife and was therefore guilty of assault.

Search and Seizure in Conjunction with an Arrest

The right of a police officer to search a prisoner at the time of arrest is conferred by the common law. This is not a blanket right to search on every occasion; however:[17]

> . . . there is no doubt that a man when in custody may so conduct himself, by reason of violence of language or conduct, that a police officer may reasonably think it prudent and right to search him . . .

Although there is a specific right in section 117.02 of the *Criminal Code* for a peace officer to search for weapons, the general right is at common law. The courts have confirmed the right of the citizen to search on arrest and the security officer would therefore have the same right.[18] A security officer would be wise to avoid a search, unless it is necessary:

- to protect the prisoner or others (*e.g.*, where there is evidence that the prisoner has a weapon); or
- to recover evidence that may be in the possession of the accused.

---

[17] *Gordon v. Denison* (1895), 22 O.A.R. 315 at p. 326 (App. Div.), revg 24 O.R. 576 (Common Pleas Div.). These words of Maclennan J.A., who dissented in this judgment on a different issue, have been quoted often.

[18] *R. v. Lerke, supra*, footnote 12.

Whenever the police are expected to immediately be involved in taking custody of a prisoner, the security officer may elect to await their arrival before conducting a search to recover evidence. If a search is improperly completed because the person arresting went beyond the bounds of authority, there is the likelihood that at trial the court will disallow any evidence obtained during the search.

SEARCHES AT THE WORKSITE

Lockers and Personal Effects

What about the right of an employer, or security staff on its behalf, to search at a worksite? As part of an investigation, these searches are usually conducted on employee lockers, lunch buckets or purses, vehicles or other personal effects. They may also be carried out in conjunction with a company policy (*e.g.*, a policy restricting drugs or alcohol at the worksite or a policy prohibiting company property from being kept in employee lockers).

The security officer is not performing a "governmental function" when conducting routine searches at the worksite and, therefore, the *Canadian Charter of Rights and Freedoms* does not apply. There have been attempts by labour unions to use the Charter as an argument to restrict security procedures, but generally the courts will weigh the public interest.[19]

Guidelines for Searches at the Worksite

- The search must be reasonable — there must be some evidence that the offence took place and that the search will provide evidence.
- The search policy should be applied consistently and should not target an individual or department.

When searches are conducted in the workplace they should be performed in a uniform manner, there should be evidence of their necessity and there should be respect for the employee's right to privacy. In an Ontario arbitration case an employee applied for and was awarded an apology from the employer when random searches were conducted of

---

[19]   In an unreported British Columbia case involving the Association of Machinists and Aerospace Workers the right of Transport Canada to conduct searches, fingerprint and carry out security checks on airport personnel was approved.

lockers, purses and personal effects.[20] Evidence indicated that the grievor was asked to pull a sweater up to her waist, empty her pockets and pull her pant legs up to the top of her socks. The search was in full view of other employees passing by. The arbitrator commented on the right of the employer to conduct searches, but held that the search should have been conducted in a manner that would have provided privacy.

Searches of Vehicles

ACME GLASS

VEHICLES WILL BE SEARCHED
UPON LEAVING COMPANY PROPERTY

The employer may set up search procedures as a condition of employment, or searches may be a condition of entering company property and a warning sign may be posted at vehicle entrances. Upon entering company property the visitor, employee or other person, in effect, voluntarily grants the company a "licence" (*i.e.*, authorization) to perform a search if security deems one necessary. However, a licence that is given can also be taken away and the person who entered the property can later decide that he or she does not wish to allow his vehicle to be searched. A forced search by security personnel once the vehicle leaves the site may result in a civil action against the company and the security staff. The incident, however, may still be recorded and handled in the following way:

---

[20] *Drug Trading Co. and ECWU, Local 11 (Re)* (1988), 32 L.A.C. (3d) 443 (Ont. Arb. Bd.).

Personnel Involved	Action
Visitor	The visitor will not be allowed back on site.
Salesperson	Advise the individual's company that the person will not be allowed back on site.
Contractors	Advise the individual's company that the person will not be allowed back on site.
Employees	Treat the issue as a disciplinary matter for failure to follow company procedures.

Searches Under Warrant

Where the police obtain a warrant to search a building, receptacle or a location, the *Criminal Code* provides that the Justice of the Peace may allow the warrant to name a person who is not a peace officer to assist the police with their search.[21] This happens when a person has expertise or a competence that the police require to effectively carry out the search. For example, in a search of a residence for the recovery of property stolen from a company, the warrant may name a security officer employed by the company to help in stolen property identification. A security officer should not assist the police with a search of private property unless:

- the property is company owned;
- the officer is specifically named in the search warrant; or
- the property owner has given him specific authority.

OTHER SECURITY CONCERNS

Wiretap Legislation

Security professionals should be aware of the provisions of wiretap legislation because:

- The corporation may be the victim of an eavesdropping attempt by an outsider whose purpose is to gain confidential information.
- Every investigator should be aware of the parameters of the privacy legislation in effect in order to ensure that such parameters are not breached in the course of an inquiry.
- The present technology located in the worksite often includes electronic monitoring of employees and the security officer should ensure that the devices used do not breach existing legislation.

---

[21] See section 487 of the *Criminal Code.*

Section 183 of the *Criminal Code* defines "private communication" as:

> . . . any oral communication, or any telecommunication . . . that is made under circumstances in which it is reasonable for the originator to expect that it will not be intercepted by any person other than the person intended by the originator to receive it . . .

A whispered conversation that is overheard is not considered to be a "private communication". The parties to the conversation ought to have known that they could be overheard. However, if an electronic device is used to amplify and pick up a whispered conversation, a *Criminal Code* privacy infraction exists.

In Canada, it is not an offence for one party to a conversation to record it without the knowledge of the other. One of the parties to a conversation can also give authority to a third party to make a recording. For example, it is not a criminal offence for a security officer to conceal a microphone to record a conversation in a room where one of the parties to that conversation has given consent. Although the consent does not have to be in writing, it should be. The police, however, must obtain legal authorization even where there is third party consent.

> *A security officer conceals a tape recorder in a briefcase and records a meeting with two suspects. During the course of the meeting the security officer excuses himself and leaves the room, but leaves the briefcase behind with the recorder still running.*

Was the recording of the conversation legal while the security officer was in the room?

Was it legal after the security officer left?

Admissibility of Wiretap Evidence at Trial

Although it may not be contrary to the *Criminal Code* to record a conversation where one party has provided consent, such a recording may still be inadmissible at trial in a civil or criminal action. The courts have become increasingly reluctant to allow taped conversations into evidence where one of the parties was unaware that the conversation was being recorded.[22]

---

[22] See *Ferguson v. McBee Technographics Inc.* (1989), 24 C.P.R. (3d) 240, [1989] 2 W.W.R. 499 (Man. Q.B.), for an example of a case where a tape-recorded telephone conversation with one-party consent was not allowed into evidence because it offended the Manitoba *Privacy Act.* In *R. v. Duarte* (1990), 65 D.L.R. (4th) 240,

Computer Crime

Computer crime can be either external or internal. External crimes typically involve either access to a computer system with the intent of using it to commit a fraud against the company or another user of the system, or hacking with the intention of creating mischief. An example of an external crime is the creation of a virus that can be lodged in a company's computer system. Internal computer fraud is the use of a computer system for the purpose of misusing computer time or for the purpose of fraud. An example of an internal computer crime is a payroll manager using the payroll software system to deposit money into his own bank account through the automatic bank deposit system. This generally involves putting terminated employees back onto the system and diverting money to the manager's own bank account that should otherwise have been transferred to Canada Customs and Revenue Agency (formerly Revenue Canada).

On occasion, the company itself may set up its computers to perpetrate a criminal activity. In one unreported case, a company set up its accounts receivable system so that when monthly invoices went out they did not show money received during the past billing period. Many customers would double pay because their invoice did not show the previous month's payment. The company pleaded guilty to fraud.

Amendments to the *Criminal Code* in 1986[23] and 1997[24] provide for five computer crime offences:

- obtaining a computer service fraudulently and without colour of right (hacking);[25]
- intercepting any function of a computer system (wiretapping);[26]
- using a computer to commit offences 1 or 2 above;[27]
- committing mischief by destroying data, rendering it meaningless or interfering with the use of data;[28]
- using, possessing or trafficking in a password to permit unauthorized use of a computer to commit an offence.[29]

---

53 C.C.C. (3d) 1 (S.C.C.), the Supreme Court of Canada held that the interception of private communications without judicial authorization even where there was one-party consent offended section 8 of the Charter.

[23] *Criminal Law Amendment Act, 1985*, R.S.C. 1985, c. 27 (1st Supp.).

[24] *Criminal Law Improvement Act, 1996*, S.C. 1997, c. 18, s. 18.

[25] Section 342.1(1)(*a*).

[26] Section 342.1(1)(*b*). See *R. v. Forsythe* (1991), 137 A.R. 321 (Prov. Ct.), for an example where a private investigator was charged under the *Criminal Code* with accessing the Canadian Police Information Centre's criminal records. Fortunately for the investigator there was insufficient evidence to pursue the charge to conviction.

[27] Section 342.1(1)(*c*).

[28] Section 430(1.1) and (5.1).

[29] Section 342.1(1)(*d*) was added by S.C. 1997, c. 18, s. 18.

"Fraudulently and without colour of right" indicates that the accused must have acted dishonestly in the sense that reasonable people familiar with the normal business dealings would find their activities to be dishonest.[30]

Note also the definitions provided in section 342.1(2) for the following terms:

- computer program
- computer service
- computer system
- data
- electro-magnetic, acoustic, mechanical or other device
- function
- intercept.

Two other sections of the *Criminal Code* relate to computer or technological crime:

- possession of a device to obtain a telecommunication facility or service (section 327); and
- theft of a telecommunication service (section 326).

Often, even though a computer crime has been committed, the prosecutor will elect to lay charges under one of the more conventional sections of the *Criminal Code* (*e.g.*, fraud). Crimes involving computers are often associated with other offences. In one unreported 1993 case involving an extortion attempt against a bank the extortionist admitted his guilt claiming to possess detailed knowledge of the bank's computer system and cabling locations.

The *Criminal Code* provides for penalties of up to 10 years in jail. Section 430 includes in the term "mischief" the offences of destroying, altering, obstructing, interrupting or interfering with data or any person in lawful use of data. That section also carries penalties of up to 10 years where prosecution is by way of indictment.

Telecommunications Fraud

Telecommunications fraud may include:

- unauthorized use of a telephone (*e.g.*, an employee uses the company telephone to make personal long distance calls);

---

[30] *R. v. Zlatic* (1993), 100 D.L.R. (4th) 642, 79 C.C.C. (3d) 466 (S.C.C.); *R. v. Théroux* (1993), 100 D.L.R. (4th) 624, 79 C.C.C. (3d) 449 (S.C.C.).

- hacking into a company system (*e.g.*, a "phreak"[31] discovers that a company telephone system still has the factory installed password and is able to use the system to make long distance calls);
- theft of a cellular phone or duplication of the electronic serial number;
- unauthorized access into a company voicemail system;[32] and
- simple theft of telephone credit cards.

Although many of these activities may constitute offences, it is often difficult for a company to prove damages or economic loss (especially in the case of access to a voicemail box) and, therefore, conviction of the accused may be impossible.

Trespass

There are three ways to deal with trespass:

- as a civil action;
- under provincial statutes (usually a petty trespass Act);
- as a *Criminal Code* violation under section 177 (trespassing at night).

The provincial trespass Acts usually contain provisions that prescribe the methods of giving notice (word of mouth, in writing, signs, etc.), the placement of signage, the powers of arrest allowed peace officers, property owners, occupiers or employees, and the fines that may be levied. The normal defence to a charge under a provincial trespass statute is a fair and reasonable supposition of right.

Attempts, Conspiracy and Counselling

Under the *Criminal Code*, someone may be charged with an attempt[33] or conspiracy to commit a criminal offence[34] even where the substantive offence did not occur. The *Code* also provides for the crime of counselling a criminal offence.[35] The charge of "conspiracy to commit" is often referred to by defence counsel as "the prosecutor's delight" because the range of evidence that may be introduced is much broader in a conspiracy

---

[31] A "phreak" (sometimes "phreaker") is a person who compromises telephone switching equipment primarily for the purpose of stealing service.

[32] Phreaks will also use automatic dialing programs to attempt to gain access to company voicemail systems or they may call employees in a company, indicate that they are the system administrator and ask for the employees' passwords. This will give them access to a voicemail box which they can then use for their own purposes.

[33] Sections 24 and 463.

[34] Section 465.

[35] Section 22.

trial than it is in a trial for the substantive offence. For example, if A conspires with B to commit an offence and B also includes C in the planning, A, B and C may be found guilty of a conspiracy even though A and C may never have met each other.

Corporate Criminal Liability

Early criminal law had a great deal of difficulty with the concept of holding a corporation liable for a criminal offence because "it has no soul to be damned and no body to be kicked".[36] Those concerns were eventually overcome with the development of the *alter ego* doctrine which stipulated that an officer, director, employee and, in some cases, a licensee may be the directing will of the corporation and the *mens rea* of that person may be imputed to be the corporate entity.[37] The *Criminal Code* has also addressed those concerns by defining "every one", "person", "owner", etc., as including "bodies corporate, societies, companies".[38]

In addition, the *Criminal Code* addresses the fact that a corporation cannot be imprisoned by providing for fines and distress warrants in lieu of sentencing.[39] The significance of corporate criminal liability is that where an employee of a company has "sole and acting directing will" for a particular area,[40] the corporation may be found criminally liable for an act of that person. If there is some form of negligence involved, the corporation may even be charged with criminal negligence or manslaughter.[41]

Bill C-45[42] provides for amendments to the *Criminal Code* to expand corporate criminal liability in matters of occupational health and safety and other criminal offences. The amendments also make it easier to convict organizations for workplace safety violations and create a new offence of criminal negligence for health and safety infractions. Before the amendments, in order to show the *mens rea* for a criminal offence, the directing mind of the organization was at a fairly high level with regard to

---

[36] This famous statement is attributed to England's eminent Lord Chancellor Edward Thurlow (1731-1806). See D.S. Shrager and E. Frost, *The Quotable Lawyer* (New York: 1986). A similar observation was made by the great English legalist Edward Coke, who wrote: "Corporations cannot commit treason, nor be outlawed, for they have no soul."

[37] *Lennard's Carrying Co. v. Asiatic Petroleum Co.*, [1915] A.C. 705 (H.L.).

[38] Section 2.

[39] Sections 735 and 734.6.

[40] *R. v. Fane Robinson Ltd.*, [1941] 3 D.L.R. 409, 76 C.C.C. 196 (Alta. C.A.).

[41] In *R. v. Syncrude Canada Ltd.*, [1984] 1 W.W.R. 355, 28 Alta. L.R. (2d) 233 (Q.B.), a corporation was charged but acquitted of criminal negligence causing death as the result of the asphyxiation deaths of two contract workers doing repair work on a vessel.

[42] *Act to Amend the Criminal Code (Criminal Liability of Organizations)*, S.C. 2003, c. 21, in force March 31, 2004.

protection from liability, but the amendments reduce that level to correspond with that of a lower-ranking individual. A company and/or an individual company official may be charged with criminal negligence if a senior officer commits the offence, directs a representative to commit the offence, fails to prevent a representative from committing an offence that the individual knew was about to occur, or demonstrates a lack of care. The amendments provide for fines of up to $100,000 against an organization and fines and/or imprisonment for up to 25 years against a senior officer.

Entrapment

The defence of "entrapment" is relatively new to Canada. The burden is on the accused to raise the defence and prove it on a balance of probabilities, which means the accused must testify. The test will be whether the police or undercover operative went beyond providing the opportunity to commit the offence and actually induced the commission of the offence. The investigator may only present the opportunity to one who arouses suspicion and may not induce the commission of the offence by pressuring, threatening or deceiving the accused. In some exceptional circumstances where entrapment is raised as a defence the prosecutor may be allowed to introduce evidence, but the investigator in the case must have been testing "an area where criminal activity was occurring".

The concern with entrapment is that an investigator may attempt to induce an otherwise innocent person to commit an offence when there was no reason to suspect the person was involved in any illegal activity. This is known as "random virtue testing"[43] and will not be admitted as evidence unless there existed a *bona fide* inquiry into probable criminal activity prior to the entrapment. When an investigator presents the opportunity to commit an offence there must be a reasonable suspicion that:

- the person is already engaged in the known or alleged criminal activity; or
- the physical location with which the person is associated is a place where the particular criminal activity is likely occurring.

The court will consider:

- the reasonableness of the suspicion;
- the availability of other investigative techniques;
- whether an average person with both the strengths and weaknesses and in the position of the accused would be induced to commit the crime;

---

[43] *R. v. Mack* (1988), 44 C.C.C. (3d) 513 (S.C.C.).

- the persistence and number of attempts by the investigator before the accused agreed to commit the offence;
- the type of inducement used by the investigator, including deceit, fraud, trickery or reward;
- the timing of the investigator's conduct and, in particular, whether the investigator instigated the offence or became involved in ongoing criminal activities;
- whether the investigator's conduct involved an exploitation of human characteristics, such as friendship;
- whether the investigator exploited a particular vulnerability of the person, such as a mental handicap or substance addiction;
- the harm caused or risk created by the investigator as compared to that caused by the accused, and the commission of illegal acts by the investigator himself;
- the existence of any threats, implied or expressly made, against the accused by the investigator or other agents; and
- whether the investigator's conduct was directed at undermining other constitutional values.[44]

Young Offenders

The *Youth Criminal Justice Act*[45] provides for the special treatment of those accused who are under 18 years of age. The Act provides for reduced maximum sentences and alternative measures for young offenders convicted of criminal offences. In addition, the Act provides for notice to be given to parents and guardians and for transfer to adult court where the alleged offences are more serious. Because the identity of young offenders is protected by law, security officers must be extra careful and protective of investigative reports involving young persons.[46]

CONCLUSION

This chapter has emphasized the importance of a thorough understanding of criminal law practice and the legality of search and seizure proce-

---

[44] In *R. v. Barnes* (1991), 63 C.C.C. (3d) 1, [1991] 1 S.C.R. 449, the Supreme Court of Canada held that the mere fact that the accused was previously involved in criminal activity was insufficient to establish "reasonable suspicion".

[45] S.C. 2002, c. 1, was brought into force April 1, 2003, to replace the *Young Offenders Act*, R.S.C. 1985, c. Y-1.

[46] For cases where security officers have been involved in the arrest of young offenders see: *R. v. C. (C.M.)*, [1991] 3 S.C.R. 683, 108 N.S.R. (2d) 359; *R. v. L. (T.)* (1996), 142 Nfld. & P.E.I.R. 103, [1996] N.J. No. 212 (QL) (Prov. Ct.); and *R. v. A. (J.)*, [1992] O.J. No. 182 (QL) (U.F. Ct.).

dures. In order to be effective, security professionals need to know the legal limits of their actions, especially with respect to the application of restraint and the conduct of investigative techniques that may require secrecy. For intelligent decisions to be made, the notions of criminal intent, indictable and non-indictable offences, notification of rights, common law powers of arrest, corporate liability and reasonable force must be mastered by practitioners in the field of security. A constant review of new trends in the law is required. As we have seen, legal notions in this country are based on precedent and precedents are shaped by the past, the present and desires for change in the future. To keep abreast of changes in the law, the assistance of legal counsel should be sought and an awareness of the security professional's role in the legal prevention and control of criminal activity should be fostered.

6

Civil Law — Effect on the Security Industry

INTRODUCTION

As we learned in Chapter 1, "Private Security Practice and the Canadian Legal System", in Canada the laws that serve to regulate everyday behaviour, ranging from our commercial interactions to our interpersonal relationships, fall into two categories — criminal law and civil law.

It is also important to recall that, in Canada, the term "civil law" has two separate and distinct meanings:

- in the province of Quebec — civil law jurisprudence developed from the Napoleonic Code and now established in the *Civil Code of Québec*;[1] or
- in the common law provinces and territories (*i.e.*, all other Canadian jurisdictions) — civil law as opposed to criminal law.

For the purposes of our discussion, we will be examining the latter application of the term. As previously noted, Canadian civil law developed in the same way as the criminal law out of the precedents set by common and case law. In some instances, civil and criminal law cases may affect each other. For example, the criminal law principle on corporate criminal liability was established in an English civil law case.[2] Both criminal and civil courts use precedents developed in relation to admissibility of evidence.

Simply stated, civil law is the area of jurisprudence that regulates the stipulated obligations between individuals and other entities (*e.g.*, corporations, government, private persons), the penalties arising from breaches

---

[1] S.Q. 1991, c. 64. First encoded as the *Civil Code of Lower Canada* (*Code civile du Bas Canada*) and renamed *Civil Code of Québec* (*Code civile du Québec*) after Confederation, it was updated and rewritten in 1991.

[2] See the discussion of the *alter ego* doctrine in Chapter 5, "Criminal Law", under the heading "Corporate Criminal Liability".

of those obligations and the enforcement of the associated penalties. Insofar as security is involved with the protection of assets, the civil law sets forth legal obligations concerned with the protection of property and/or the safeguarding of human or other resources within a corporation. As a result, the security department becomes involved in commitments that will have repercussions on areas of liability to the corporation and on the human relations issues between the corporation and its employees.

The intent of this chapter, therefore, is to provide the reader with a basis for understanding the role that the civil law plays in the performance of security work.

MAJOR AREAS OF THE CIVIL LAW

There are three major areas of the civil law:

1. *Purely civil* — It protects the private rights of the individual, is based on the common law and has not been legislated by statute (*e.g.*, torts, contracts and trusts).
2. *Quasi-civil* — It protects the private rights of the individual and is governed by statute (*e.g.*, civil and regulatory agencies created by statute — corporate, family and property law).
3. *Cross-jurisdictional* — It covers both criminal and civil law (*e.g.*, securities and environmental legislation).

ADMINISTRATIVE LAW

Administrative law falls within the broad umbrella of civil law but relates specifically to the rules governing relationships between the government and its citizens. The definition of "administrative law" is a "body of principles and rules stating and governing the functions and powers of all agencies of government concerned with the application, working out and practical administration of government policy".[3]

The area of administrative law is becoming more and more important because of the development of tribunals and regulatory bodies to govern the relationships between private citizens and businesses, and businesses with each other in Canada today. Examples of tribunals are:

-   Ministries of the Crown;
-   public corporations;
-   labour relations tribunals;

---

[3]   D.M. Walker, *The Oxford Companion to the Law* (Oxford: Clarendon Press, 1980), at p. 27.

- municipal tribunals;
- vocational tribunals; and
- immigration tribunals.

An example within the security industry is the existence of provincial bodies that provide licensing and regulation of the industry. Administrative law principles would apply where someone was turned down for a security licence or where there was an application for the revocation of a licence by the provincial body.

Tribunals have broader powers than the courts, and for that reason administrative law principles are important to the definition of those powers. They include:

- rules of interpretation;
- entry and inspection;
- obtaining the release of information;
- available remedies; and
- prosecutorial discovery.

Consider, for example, the broad power of fire inspectors to enter and inspect premises, the powers of human rights tribunals to order companies to create policies and training programs, and the right of Canada Customs and Revenue Agency to demand documents and records.

The major issues in administrative law are how far, by what means and in what circumstances will courts intervene to control or overrule a tribunal.

Tribunals must ensure that the right of a citizen to be heard is protected; on the other hand, when the issue is purely investigative in nature, there is no requirement that a hearing be convened. Tribunal hearings are not bound by the formal procedures of the courts of law and may develop their own procedures. For the tribunal to arrive at a *quasi*-judicial disposition a fairness test must apply — in other words, the issue at hand must not be contrary to the code of natural justice. Natural justice, in this case, simply means "fair play".

As a general rule, there is no appeal from a tribunal decision except where it is allowed by statute, although some common law exceptions to the general rule do exist. The exceptions may be brought forward in the form of:

- *habeas corpus* — an order that the person subject to the tribunal's decision be brought before the court to review the legality of the decision;
- *certiorari* — a review for:
  - a jurisdictional error, abuse or denial,

- • an error in law on the record,
- • fraud, or
- • bias by the tribunal;
- *mandamus* — a writ of instruction by a higher court to a lower court to perform a duty it has failed to perform;
- *quo warranto* — *ultra vires* — "Under what warrant?" is used where the actions of the tribunal may be "outside their authority";
- declaration — an application to a higher court or tribunal;
- injunction — usually used as an application to a court to stop a tribunal from proceeding;
- damages — where the actions of the tribunal have caused an unjustifiable loss.

Regulatory or Public Welfare Offences

Most offences in the *Criminal Code* are true crimes — the prosecutor must show *mens rea* in order to convict the accused. There are a few offences in the *Code* that are strict liability offences — where the onus of proof shifts to the accused.[4] Some sections, although there is no onus that shifts to the accused, may be based on negligence. In proving a case of impaired driving, for example, the prosecutor need not show that the accused deliberately drove while impaired, thus the only *mens rea* to the offence is driving the vehicle while impaired.[5]

Many regulatory offences, however, are considered absolute liability offences where guilt can be established without either *mens rea* or proof of intentional negligence on the part of the accused. An example is environmental legislation where a company spills a toxic substance into the environment. The company may be convicted and fined in spite of the fact that the offence was not committed deliberately and in spite of the fact that negligence could not be proved with respect to the manner in which the toxic substance was handled.

Burden of Proof

$$\longrightarrow$$

Mens rea	Strict Liability	Absolute Liability
true crime	based on negligence	liability regardless of intention or negligence

---

[4]   See, for example, section 351 of the *Criminal Code* (possession of housebreaking instruments). Simple possession of such tools creates a presumption of intent to commit a crime that an accused would be hard-pressed to disprove.

[5]   Criminal negligence causing death or causing bodily harm (sections 220 and 221) are other examples.

The only defences to absolute liability offences are the *actus reus* defences — duress, infancy, automatism, insanity, sabotage, or an act of God. There is also a common law defence of *de minimus non curat lex* ("the law will not consider trifles") which, when successful, allows the accused to establish that the offence was so minimal that it should not be put before the court.

CONTRACT LAW AND SECURITY SERVICES

Security services are often contracted to private corporations by private security agencies or agent(s). A "contract" is an agreement between two or more competent parties in which an offer is made and accepted and each party benefits (*e.g.*, a commissionaire is contracted to patrol a building). Alternatively, a contract may also be an agreement between two or more competent parties that creates obligations to do or not do the specific things that are the subject of that agreement (*e.g.*, a contract is signed with an alarm company to install security alarms in a company's corporate headquarters).

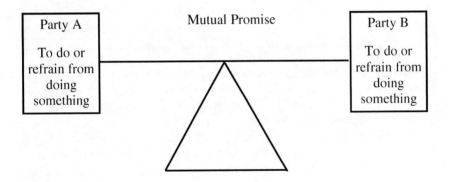

Express Contract

In an express contract, the terms and conditions are stated in words. If, during the negotiations for the purchase of an access control system, for example, the vendor agrees to provide a certain model at a certain price by an assigned date and the security director agrees to pay the price, an express contract has been put into effect.

Implied Contract

In an implied contract, the terms and conditions are not stated in words but can be assumed from the actions of the parties. These contracts may be implied in law or in fact.

Contract Implied in Law	Contract Implied in Fact
The law implies there exists agreement or obligation of one party to another where there has been a benefit. It has a common basis in equity and the rule against one person being unjustly enriched at the expense of another. For example, a customer sits down in a restaurant and orders a meal. There is a civil law obligation to pay for the meal even though the customer may never have said, "If you prepare a meal for me, I will pay you for it."	The obligation of one party to another can be implied from the facts, even though there are no formal words of agreement. For example, a security department with a large inventory of CCTV equipment calls its supplier and asks that three more cameras be sent over as soon as possible. Although no offer to supply the cameras came from the supplier and no payment was offered by the security director at the time, the request itself implies there is agreement to pay for these goods if and when they are delivered.

On the other hand, if a critical term is omitted from an agreement the courts will not find an implied contract to exist. For example, a corporation negotiates with a guard company for the supply of uniformed officers. They may discuss price per hour, but if there is no discussion about the number of guards that will be needed or when they are to start, etc., no implied contract is considered to exist. The essential elements of quantity and time of performance are missing and no real negotiations can be considered to have taken place.

The courts will sometimes impose a term or condition on an implied contract. Assume a corporation and a guard company enter into negotiations and discuss the number of shifts, start date, etc., but do not address the issue of price per hour to be charged to the corporation. The guard company provides the service but when the invoice is sent out there is a dispute over the amount charged and the corporation refuses to pay. The courts may look at what is the "reasonable value" of the services rendered. In attempting to set a price the courts may look at the guard agency's overhead, usual profits on similar contracts and what is typically charged for similar agreements. It may then impose the hourly rate on the parties as part of the implied contract. In a contract implied in fact there is clear agreement between the parties to provide and pay for the service at an unstated price. The unstated price will be converted to a reasonable value by the courts.

Precautionary Measures for Managing Contracts

There are some simple precautions that should be followed in order to avoid a conflict between two parties who may be negotiating a contract:

1. Whenever possible, agreements should be in writing. Most provinces have a statute of frauds which stipulates that some agreements are not enforceable unless they are in writing:
   - those not to be completed within one year;
   - those to make good the debt of another; and
   - those relating to real property.
2. Once an agreement is in writing, it should only be changed in writing. The courts are reluctant to accept evidence of an oral change to a written document because if it was important enough to reduce to writing initially, any amendments should be also be put down on paper.

A contract will not be enforceable if it is for an illegal purpose. For example, if an investigator is hired to do illegal wiretaps the courts would not enforce the contract because it violates the *Criminal Code*.

WARRANTIES

Warranties are like contracts in that they are an agreement by the supplier of goods or services that if the purchaser buys its product it will be fit for the use intended. The difference is that a warranty is a contract with the whole world because it is enforceable against the warrantor (the manufacturer or supplier of the service) by anyone who relied on the statements related to the goods or services.

For example, a surveillance camera is sold by the manufacturer to a wholesaler, by the wholesaler to a retailer, by the retailer to an installer and by the installer to a customer. The manufacturer will be liable under warranty to the customer even though they have never dealt with each other.

The other major difference between a contract and a warranty is that, in a contract, the parties are only responsible for damages equal to the reasonable value of the goods or services provided. If a person contracts for the purchase of a fire extinguisher and the building catches fire and the extinguisher fails, the supplier is responsible only for the value of the fire extinguisher that did not work. If the purchaser is successful in an action under warranty for the failure of the extinguisher the supplier may be responsible for damages up to the value of the building that burned down because the extinguisher did not work. Warranty obviously has an important impact in the security industry where goods and services are often provided for the protection of life and property.

In order to protect themselves against this significant liability, manufacturers and providers of security services and equipment will often rely on specific language in a contract to limit their liability.

Example of a Clause in a Central Station Alarm Contract Limiting Liability

It is understood that the contractor (alarm company) is not an insurer, that insurance, if any, shall be obtained by the subscriber and that the amounts payable to the contractor hereunder are based upon the value of the services and the scope of the liability as herein set forth and are unrelated to the value of the subscriber's property or the property of others located in the subscriber's premises. The contractor makes no guarantee or warranty of merchantability or fitness, that the system or services supplied will avert or prevent occurrences or the consequences therefrom, which the system or services are designed to detect. The subscriber does not desire this contract to provide for full liability for loss or damage due directly or indirectly to occurrences, or consequences therefrom, which the service is designed to detect or avert. The subscriber further agrees that, if the contractor should be found liable for loss or damage due to a failure of service or equipment in any respect, *its liability shall be equal to a sum equal to ten per cent of the annual service charge or $250 whichever is the greater*, as the exclusive remedy and that the provisions of this paragraph shall apply if loss or damage, irrespective of cause or origin, results directly or indirectly to person or property from performance or non-performance of obligation imposed by this contract or from negligence, active or otherwise, of the contractor, or its agents or employees.

Consider by way of example the following case study where a contract exists that includes the limitation of liability clause outlined above:

A bank negotiates with an alarm company to provide alarm services for a branch vault. The equipment installed by the alarm company does not meet the standards called for in the contract (for example CSA approved). A break-in and safe robbery occurs at the branch and the equipment fails to detect the burglars. The bank sues the alarm company and proves in court:

- *that the installation did not meet the agreed standards of CSA-approved equipment; and*
- *that, as a result of the failure of the equipment, the burglary went undetected and the bank lost cash.*

At trial, the alarm company introduces the contract with the limitation of liability clause. The bank would be successful in an action against the alarm company for breach of contract (in failing to provide the proper equipment), but the bank would only be awarded an amount equal to 10% of the annual service charge or $250, whichever is greater. If the clause had not been in the contract, the alarm company may have been liable for the total amount of damages to the bank including the lost cash, damage to property as a result of the break-in and any other damages sued for and deemed appropriate.

AGENCY AND LIABILITY FOR SECURITY SERVICES

Agency addresses the question of whether a person is acting for or on behalf of someone else and it is an important consideration in assessing liability in the security environment.

How Agency is Determined

There are many situations in which one person acts on behalf of another:

- a lawyer acting on behalf of a client;
- a trustee acting on behalf of a bankrupt estate;
- an executor acting on behalf of the estate of a deceased person.

In each of these matters, the person is acting in his or her own right on behalf of the interests of another. The significance of the agency relationship is that the person's authority to act is as an extension of the employer or property owner's authority; in other words, "agency" is an extension of the master-servant principle. The general rule is that one is not responsible for the acts of a private contractor. However, there are so many exceptions that this principle is barely a rule at all. The exceptions include cases where:

- the task is performed on the land of the principal;
- specific instructions are provided on how to perform the task;
- the task is inherently dangerous.

Where plaintiffs wish to add the principal to a lawsuit (usually because there is a better chance of collecting damages), they may be successful by arguing one or more of the following principles:

- express appointment;
- ratification of actions taken;
- apparent authority.

Express Appointment

In an express appointment, the principal (company owner) or employer defines the tasks of the agent or employee. This is the normal situation in a contractual employment relationship, labour agreement, or employment at will. In most employment relationships the employer has defined the duties of the agent or employee with verbal instructions, or written policies and procedures. For example, it is common procedure for a large guard operation to post orders that outline guard responsibilities. As long as the guards are acting within the scope of the posted orders there is an agency relationship between the guards and the company contracting for their services.

Ratification of Actions Taken

An agency relationship may also develop where there was no verbal or written extension of the employer's authority but the employer later ratifies or condones an action that has occurred (even if the employer was unaware of the action at the time it took place).

> *A visitor to a site is stopped at the gate on leaving and is asked to open the trunk of his vehicle. He refuses. The contract guard leaves the gate down so that the visitor cannot drive out. The guard uses a pry bar to open the vehicle trunk. The visitor sues the guard company and the company operating the site for the damage to his vehicle. In response to the civil action, the company provides a statement of defence that this is the standard operating procedure undertaken when an individual refuses a request from the guard to open the vehicle's trunk for a search before exiting the site.*

The company owning the property has established an agency relationship between itself and the guard because of the ratification of his actions.

Apparent Authority

Apparent authority can exist where the company:

- is in a position to know the actions of the agent;
- does not disclaim the actions of the agent; and
- puts the agent in a position where the agent appears to act on the company's behalf.

> *A guard accepts a package from a visitor for safekeeping even though there are specific instructions not to accept packages. The package goes missing and is established to have a great deal of value. The visitor sues the company for the value of the package. The visitor had no knowledge of the fact that the guard should not have accepted the package, and the guard was apparently acting on behalf of the company in accepting it. If the visitor can prove negli-*

gence then he has a good chance of recovering against the company because the package was accepted for safekeeping by the guard in the course of his duties.

The Importance of Agency

If there is a wrongful act on the part of someone who can be established as an agent of the organization (because of express appointment, ratification of actions taken or apparent authority to act), the organization may be held liable for the acts of the agent. Normally, the organization need only be concerned where the acts of the agent are negligent or there is an intentional wrong. However, in situations involving inherently dangerous work (as is usually found in security operations), the employer may also be found liable for the unintentional wrongs of the agent because greater care should have been taken to determine the character of and in supervision of the agent hired to perform the duties.

Organizations can protect themselves against the acts of contract agents by ensuring there are indemnity or "hold harmless" clauses in the contracts entered into and by ensuring there are provisions requiring that the contractors engaged possess adequate liability insurance.

Vicarious Liability

Vicarious liability is the foundation of the agency relationship. It exists when one person is liable for the negligent actions or conduct of another, even though the first person was not directly responsible for the harmful act or misconduct of the other. It is based on the concept that a principal (*e.g.*, a business owner) may be liable for the wrong done by an agent where that agent is acting within the scope of company authority. In a civil action for negligence or the intentional wrongful act of a contracted agent, the plaintiff will likely sue the agent, the agent's employer and the company that contacted the agent. The wrongful act of a contract guard, for example, may result in an action against the guard personally, the guard company and the company that contracted with the guard company. The plaintiff will realize that he is unlikely to collect a large damages award from the guard and that it is in his best interests to establish that there was an agency relationship with the guard company and the contracting company because there is more likelihood of collecting damages.

Liability and the Security Industry

The nature of the security industry is such that there is a significant exposure to the risk of serious liability. The security industry deals with protection of life and property and liability may arise as a result of negligent advice or a failure to protect. Liability may also arise as a result of the failure to properly conduct an investigation assigned to a company's security department or contracted to an outside investigator. Consider the following scenarios:

- Security recommends that an area be fenced to restrict access to the property. Management decides not to fence the area and a trespasser comes onto the property and assaults an employee.
- An apartment dweller has valuables stolen from the residence. There have been several complaints by residents about strangers in the building and several requests for video camera surveillance and front door monitors.
- A female staying in a hotel is sexually assaulted in her room. The assailant was able to get a key for the room from the front desk by stating that he had left his key in the room. There is no other security in the hotel.
- An executive is kidnapped while on business in Colombia. He was not given any instructions on the risk of traveling in that country and the company had no contingency plan in place to deal with the incident.
- In a pre-employment investigation, a member of the security department identifies an applicant as having a criminal record when, in fact, he has confused this individual with another person with a similar name. The applicant sues for slander.

These are just a few examples of the liability that may arise from security issues within the organization. Some countermeasures can be put in place to reduce the liability of an organization in security issues. These include performing due diligence (discussed later in this chapter) and risk analysis, ensuring the company takes action where there is behaviour that requires intervention and that employees, visitors and others are properly warned of any risks they may encounter. The organization can also avoid liability by taking adequate security measures on site and adopting appropriate hiring practices. It can, of course, acquire liability insurance to reduce the amount of damages it would have to pay should there be an event.

Due diligence looks at the question of whether the person or company knew or ought to have known that there was some level of risk. It is incumbent upon the security department to do ongoing risk analysis and provide advice on countermeasures. Historical surveys and a review of community standards are important because in a litigation action the company will be asked in discovery whether there is any history of similar loss or events. The company may be liable, even when they do not have a history of similar events, if there is a history of loss in similar industries.

There are three convenience food stores on opposite corners in a downtown area. Two of the stores have had a rash of robberies but the third store is incident free and consequently the company has done nothing to introduce robbery prevention programs. The third store finally has a robbery and a customer and the clerk are badly injured. The customer sues the store for damages as a result of injuries and lost time at his professional practice. At trial, the lawyer for the customer introduces the rash of robberies at the neighbouring stores and argues that the company knew or should have known that there was a risk and should have put a robbery prevention program in place.

Policies and Procedures

Policies and procedures have a role to play in defence to litigation. If a company is able to produce documents showing that it was making attempts to reduce risk, it is in a better position to defend itself. In the convenience food store example cited above, if the company was able to establish that it had robbery prevention procedures in place it would be in a position to present them in evidence at trial.

Reports

Reports are a two-edged sword in litigation. If they are accurate and thorough they can be presented at trial to show that the company did an in-depth investigation or review and considered all of the issues. Reports can be a detriment to litigation, however, if:

- the report is inaccurate and does not cover all of the relevant facts;
- it makes bad recommendations;
- it makes libelous remarks that cannot be proven; or
- it makes recommendations that were not implemented.

CORPORATE LIABILITY

Critical Areas

The liability of corporations will vary with the type of industry and with events that may be taking place. Some examples of critical operations and events are:

Operations	Events
• hospitals and clinics • animal research facilities • information systems • schools • penitentiaries • retail and banking • parking • public service • operations with high levels of staff turnover (because of the need to train)	• trigger situations—disciplinary actions, terminations, strikes and closures. • disgruntled employees, customers or families • poor economy • downsizing and layoffs • denied promotions, short-term disability, long-term disability, workers' compensation benefits • toxic work culture or environment • inadequate site protection or security • history of security incidents including sabotage and terrorism

Possible Areas of Negligence

"An employer's duty is to avoid anything which tends to increase the risk of accident. He must foresee not only habitual but possible causes of accident and he is bound to take appropriate steps to avert them. It is the employer's duty to protect employees, even against their own imprudence, neglect, weakness and want of skill."[6]

Negligent Hiring

The elements of negligent hiring are:

• The damage was caused by an employee of the defendant.
• The employee was unfit for employment.
• The employer knew or should have known that the employee was unfit.
• The plaintiff was injured by the employee's act during contact with the employee that was connected to the employment.
• The employer owed a duty of care to the plaintiff.
• The hiring of the employee was the proximate cause of the injuries to the plaintiff.

The company may be able to defend itself if it can show a reasonable pre-hiring investigation. The reasonableness of the investigation will

---

[6]   *Canadian Encyclopedic Digest (Western)*, Volume 25, p. 361.

depend upon the nature of the position and the degree of risk associated with it.

The questions that a company may wish to ask are:

- Do we have a hiring policy and procedures?
- Are they followed on a consistent basis?
- Are our hiring practices complete and thorough?
- How can they be changed to ensure that we know who we are hiring and that they will be a fit for the job?

Negligent Retention

The elements of negligent retention are:

- The employee is hired.
- The employer becomes aware after the hiring that the employee is potentially dangerous.
- The employer retains the employee knowing of the danger.
- The plaintiff's contact with the potentially dangerous employee was connected in some way with the employment relationship.

The test that a company will have to meet is whether some reasonable action was taken once the employer became aware of the danger.

Questions that a company should ask are:

- Do we have a policy on workplace violence?
- Is that policy followed on a consistent basis?
- Do we have an awareness program to:
  - indicate zero tolerance of workplace violence?
  - instruct on the necessity and measures to report incidents?
- Do we have investigative procedures to follow up on reports?
- Do we take action or is there sometimes a tendency to sweep things under the rug?

Duty to Maintain a Safe Work Environment

Occupational health and occupiers' liability legislation requires that a company provide a safe environment for workers and visitors. A company should ask:

- Do we encourage employees to confidentially report any threats, strange behaviour, intimidation or acts of violence?
- Do we undertake security surveys and identify potential risk?
- Do we have a crisis management program in place?

Duty to Warn

There is a duty to warn those who may be put at risk. In litigation, the court will ask: "Would I want to know about it if I were a customer or an employee?" By way of example, Pan American airlines was warned by the United States government about the threat of a bomb on a United States carrier just prior to the Lockerbie tragedy. The failure to warn passengers that there was a threat concerning a bomb became an issue in the subsequent litigation and led to the eventual demise of Pan American.

If the answer to the above question is "yes", issue a warning even where it seems obvious.

Failure to Document Behaviour

In an action arising out of the negligence or poor behaviour of an employee, litigation will raise the question as to whether the behaviour was documented. For example, in a dismissal of an employee for theft and a subsequent wrongful dismissal action or arbitration, any previous discipline of the employee will become an issue. If there was a failure to document the behaviour it will either not be admissible or it will not carry the same weight as documented evidence.

A company should ask:

- In employee appraisals do we have a tendency to accentuate the positive?
- Do supervisors believe that empowerment includes letting employees work out their own personal problems even if they may be affecting work?
- Does the squeaky wheel in the organization get the grease?

What Juries and Judges Will Consider

Juries and judges are human. Whenever a large corporation is on trial, they will consider issues such as:

- the fact that the corporation has deep pockets;
- the company is probably insured for any damages;
- someone has to pay.

They also tend to be generous in their interpretation of "in the course of employment".

> *In a United States case an employee traveled to Israel for a two-week business trip. On the weekend he went on a sightseeing bus trip. The bus was bombed by terrorists and he was killed. In an action by the family against the company, the court held that the employee was killed in the course of employment in spite of the fact that it was his day off and he was on a personal excursion.*

Negligence and Factors Affecting Liability

The general principle is that you are at risk of liability for any injury arising out of a dangerous condition of which you are, or should be aware.

Due Diligence

Due diligence is a duty to stay informed about your business — political, societal, internal and external — in order to show that all precautionary steps have been taken to avoid negligence or negative consequences to operational activities. Companies should not only rely on internal expertise, but should obtain expert advice where necessary.

Foreseeability

The measure of whether the company "should have known" that a risk will cause damages will include a review of the worksite and similar incidents in similar worksites. If there is evidence of risk at any of those sites the company is likely to be considered "on notice".

Curtis v. Beatrice Foods Co.[7] is a U.S. case in which a company was able to show that it had taken a number of security measures and was not liable when an employee was kidnapped in South America. The company had warned the employee of the danger, conducted security seminars and briefings, hired an experienced negotiator after the kidnapping and displayed diligence in pursuing negotiations.

TORTS

A "tort" is defined as "a civil wrong for which the remedy is a common law action for unliquidated damages and which is not exclusively the breach of a contract or the breach of a trust or other merely equitable obligation".[8] A tort is an act that results in some form of injury or damages to another person and for which the injured person may sue the wrongdoer for the damages suffered. Some acts may be both torts and crimes; for example, in the case of battery the wrongdoer may face both civil and criminal penalties.

Torts are classified as either intentional torts or negligence. With intentional torts, the action results from a deliberate act. In negligence, there is a failure to use due care and attention.

---

[7]   481 F. Supp. 1275 (S.D.N.Y. 1980), affd 622 F.2d 203 (2nd Cir. 1980).

[8]   R.F.V. Heuston and R.S. Chambers, *Salmond & Heuston on the Law of Torts*, 19th ed. (London: Sweet & Maxwell, 1987), at p. 12.

Intentional Torts

Intentional torts occur where the actor intended the consequences of the act or, at the least, believed that the consequences were virtually certain to result from it. It is not necessary that the actor desired the consequences. If a person plants a bomb in an office complex with the intention of killing the company president but the president is away when the bomb goes off and the secretary is killed, he is still liable for the intentional tort or criminal act. He ought to have known that there would be other people on the premises at the time of detonation such that the secretary's death was a natural consequence of his act.

The following are some types of common law intentional torts that are actionable in Canada:

- *Assault* — Offensive contact or some act causing imminent apprehension of offensive contact. There need not be actual physical contact.
- *Battery* — Actual harmful contact.
- *Intentional infliction of mental suffering* — Deliberate action resulting in severe emotional distress.
- *Wrongful imprisonment* — Sometimes referred to as false arrest. Wrongful imprisonment takes place where a person is constrained without justification. It is the prevention of someone from leaving the place they are in.
- *Conversion* — Conversion is the appropriation of or intentional exercise of control over the property of another without the authority of the owner of the property. It is the civil law counterpart of theft.
- *Nuisance* — Private nuisance is the interference with the use or enjoyment of the property of another. Public nuisance is the interference with a public convenience or welfare (for example, a highway).
- *Fraud* — Deceit and injurious falsehood. It is the civil law counterpart of criminal fraud.
- *Negligent misstatement* — An action where there is economic loss as a result of a misstatement by the defendant even though there was no contract.
- *Dangerous premises* — Injury suffered while on the premises of another as a result of their dangerous state.
- *Defamation* — Either an oral (slander) or written (libel) defamatory statement. The plaintiff must prove two things: firstly, that the statement is untrue and, secondly, that it caused damage. Certain situations are not actionable:
    - statements made in Parliament (parliamentary privilege);
    - statements made between a solicitor and client in contemplation of litigation;

- in some circumstances, business reports that may be libelous but are made under a duty and without malice. This is referred to as "qualified privilege".
- *Malicious prosecution* — Proceedings instituted in malice in a criminal action, arrest or other action against the plaintiff.

Negligence

Negligence cases do not fit within specific classes of actions as do intentional torts. They have more to do with the facts surrounding them and the evidence that has been gathered. The existence of negligence is a matter of fact to be decided by a judge or jury. Thus lawyers tend to talk about negligence cases in terms of specific situations (*e.g.*, automobile accidents, medical malpractice, etc.).

DAMAGES

There are six specific categories of damages that a court may award as a result of a tort or negligence action:

- *Special damages* — Awarded for actual and quantifiable losses, *e.g.*, medical expenses, loss of income, etc.
- *General damages* — Awarded where losses are actual but more difficult to quantify, *e.g.*, pain and suffering, mental anguish, etc.
- *Contemptuous damages* — Awarded where the judge or jury finds that the plaintiff has a legitimate cause of action but it should never have been brought to court (usually $1).
- *Nominal damages* — A small sum awarded in recognition of a legal right having been violated but not intended as compensation for loss.
- *Punitive* or *exemplary damages* — A sum in excess of actual losses awarded where the defendant caused insult or outrage to the plaintiff.
- *Specific performance damages* — Usually awarded in the form of a direction to the defendant to meet contractual obligations. It will not be awarded where it would not be appropriate to force the contract to continue. For example, in a breach of a contract to install an alarm system the court would not order the contractor defendant to install the system because he is not likely to do a good job.

AVOIDING LITIGATION

Before the litigation process is initiated the aggrieved party will have to consider whether to settle without the necessity of going to court and, if not, whether the defendant will have sufficient funds to pay if damages are awarded. The plaintiff will also have to consider whether the cost of suing will exceed the amount of the loss.

The Litigation Process

Once the decision to sue is made, the plaintiff will have to decide:

- What is the cause of action?
- Can the suit be brought in Small Claims Court? The maximum amount allowable in Small Claims Court varies from province to province, but even if the amount owed is more than the maximum, the plaintiff can forgive the amount in excess of what is allowed.
- Are the limitation dates exceeded? (Limitation dates — the time limits within which a suit must be commenced — vary with the jurisdiction and the cause of action.)
- How much and what kind of damages should be claimed?
- Who will the plaintiff sue? Individuals, companies?
- What evidence is available to prove the case?

Initiating the Action

Depending on the province, the action is initiated by filing a statement of claim. The defendant then has a short period of time to file a statement of defence and, depending on the circumstances, may also file a counterclaim. If a counterclaim is filed the plaintiff will have to file a statement of defence on the counterclaim. In very specific cases where there are quantifiable damages (*e.g.*, default on a loan), the court may order summary judgment.

If the matter is contested, each party may file for discovery (compulsory full disclosure of all facts and documents on which each party relies, including affidavits from witnesses). The plaintiff and the defendant (company officials in the case of a corporation) may also be examined under oath and the questions asked and answers given may be admitted as evidence, if there is a trial. The document discovery process is the provision to the other party of all documents (except those where privilege may apply) related to the litigation. Either party can choose to enter them as exhibits. For example, if an employee is investigated for an expense account fraud and terminated, the employee, on an action for wrongful dismissal, has the right to request his personnel file and any investigation reports. Once the process is completed, the parties file a Certificate of Readiness and a trial date is set.

Costs

Costs are usually awarded to the party who wins the case; however, the costs recovered are seldom equal to the costs incurred in the action. Schedules for cost awards are established under the Rules of Court of the pertinent jurisdiction and are often only 20% to 30% of the actual costs. The court may order costs on a party-and-party basis, in which case they will be very close to the actual costs incurred.

Collecting on a Judgment

If damages are awarded, the successful party files the judgment and a writ of execution. The sheriff or bailiff service can then assist with any necessary seizure or garnishment, or the successful litigant may decide to postpone collection and wait for future assets of the losing party to materialize.

Restitution or Compensation — Recovery of Damages

Security may be in a position to help a corporation avoid costly litigation where the actions of an accused have caused a monetary loss. Through liaison with the police and the prosecutor or through civil actions there may be an opportunity to recover damages.

Criminal Code Restitutions

Under section 738 of the *Criminal Code*, the prosecutor may, on sentencing, make application for an order of restitution to the victim of the full amount of the loss. By section 739 the court may issue an order that an innocent third party, who for valuable consideration acquired property that had been obtained as a result of the commission of an offence, be compensated by the offender (*e.g.*, an innocent party who buys stolen goods that are subsequently returned to the rightful owner). Section 741 states that the party who is granted the restitution order may file it in a civil court as a judgment. They do not have to file a statement of claim or prove their case as it becomes an automatic judgment and they can immediately initiate the civil recovery process.

Civil Orders

There are two civil interlocutory orders that are important in the recovery process for corporations. The first type is the *Anton Piller* order that originated in the United Kingdom.[9] It is an ancillary order that allows for seizure, inspection and/or preservation of possibly incriminating documents or property in danger of being disposed of — basically a civil search warrant that permits a plaintiff's representative to enter premises for inspection. *Anton Piller* orders are now widely used in Canada.[10]

---

[9]   *Anton Piller KG v. Manufacturing Processes Ltd.*, [1976] 1 All E.R. 779 (C.A.).
[10]   See *Grenzservice Speditions Ges.m.b.H. v. Jans* (1995), 129 D.L.R. (4th) 733, 64 C.P.R. (3d) 129 (B.C.S.C.); *Girocredit Bank Aktiengesellscaft Der Sparkassen v. Bader*, [1996] B.C.J. No. 479 (QL) (B.C.S.C.), vard 178 W.A.C. 19 (C.A.), leave to appeal to S.C.C. refused 206 W.A.C. 282n, 236 N.R. 192n *sub nom. Girocredit*

A software company has information that an organization is using boot-legged copies of its product. They obtain an Anton Piller order to allow them to go into the defendant's premises and search for the bootlegged software.

The second type of order is the *Mareva* injunction.[11] Originally this allowed the plaintiff to freeze assets before a trial or judgment in the case. The plaintiff had to show that there was a genuine risk of the goods or property being disposed of or moved outside the jurisdiction. The defendant's assets would then be frozen by the court pending disposition.[12] Today, a *Mareva* injunction generally takes the form of a remedy designed to obtain something like security, by at least ensuring there are funds available to meet any judgment, but such injunction does not create a proprietary right in enjoined property.

TRUSTS

Trusts are the third area of purely civil law. Most litigation in this field relates to the trustee relationship set up by an estate in a will. A trust may also be created in a professional relationship, such as a lawyer or realtor holding funds for a client. Section 336 of the *Criminal Code* allows for actions for breach of trust.

SECURITY INDUSTRY REGULATION

Legislation governing the security industry was first introduced in 1964 and, at present, all provinces have regulating statutes. The purpose of the legislation is to ensure that the public can rely on the good character of individuals providing security services. This is achieved through:

- investigation provisions for applicants;
- licensing;
- minimum age requirements;
- criminal records checks;
- stipulations on the types of uniforms that may be used;

Bank v. Bader; and *Davidson v. Hyundai Auto Canada Inc.*, [1988] O.J. No. 276 (QL) (S.C.).

[11] *Mareva Compania Naviera S.A. v. International Bulkcarriers Ltd.*, [1975] 2 Lloyd's Rep. 509 (C.A.).

[12] See *Z Ltd. v. A-Z and AA-LL*, [1982] Q.B. 558 (C.A.); *Babanaft International Co. S.A. v. Bassatne*, [1989] 1 All E.R. 433 (C.A.); *Aetna Financial Services v. Feigelman* (1985), 15 D.L.R. (4th) 161, 4 C.P.R. (3d) 145 (S.C.C.); *Mooney v. Orr* (1994), 33 C.P.C. (3d) 13, [1995] 1 W.W.R. 517 (B.C.S.C.).

- bonding requirements; and
- provisions for investigating complaints.

In-house security people are not regulated by any of the provincial statutes, although regulation has been considered in some provinces.

INTELLECTUAL PROPERTY

Intellectual property is an area of law that covers a number of intangible and exclusive rights. The value of intellectual property derives from the information used to develop creative or new commercially viable ideas. Intellectual property protections provide a way to safeguard from exploitation and theft those individuals and entities, including commercial enterprises, who have developed ideas, inventions and creative expression. These rights give intellectual property owners the right to exclude others from access to or use of such information or ideas. In order to prosper many companies today depend on the ideas, systems, technological breakthroughs and methods that are developed within their facilities. Because of the enormous potential value of new developments, especially in the areas of engineering, entertainment and scientific research, the prevention of intellectual property theft is an increasingly challenging job and one that security workers must take very seriously.

Intellectual property rights include:

- *Copyright* — Rights relative to literary and artistic work. Copyright is important in a security program, especially as it relates to protection of the copyright on computer software.[13]
- *Patents* — Rights in respect of inventions. Security is often charged with the protection of research and development work while it is in the early stages and prior to filing for a patent.[14]
- *Trade secrets* — Provide for the protection of work in process from misuse or abuse by employees who have a duty of confidentiality.
- *Trade-marks* — Marks used to distinguish wares or services. Security is often charged with the investigation of misuse of a trade-mark or the illegal manufacturing of "knock off" items.[15]
- *Industrial designs* — Shapes, patterns or ornamentation applied to an industrially produced object.

---

[13] Copyright in Canada is regulated by the *Copyright Act*, R.S.C. 1985, c. C-42.

[14] Patents in Canada are regulated by the *Patent Act*, R.S.C. 1985, c. P-4.

[15] Trade-marks in Canada are governed by the *Trade-marks Act*, R.S.C. 1985, c. T-13.

- *Integrated circuit topographies* — Three-dimensional configurations of the electronic circuits embodied in integrated circuit products or layout designs.

Copyright

Copyright, the widest form of intellectual property, includes plans, engineering drawings, notes, musical, artistic and literary works. Copyright in Canada is automatic, although minimal requirements must be met for a work to be copyrighted. The work must:

- be original (but not necessarily new);
- be fixed in tangible form (*e.g.*, paper or disc);
- demonstrate a minimum level of creativity; and
- be of Canadian origin. (The statute at section 5(1)(*a*) states "the author was, at the date of the making of the work, a citizen or subject of, or a person ordinarily resident in a treaty country" — in this case, Canada. The "treaty" is the *Berne Convention*.[16])

With respect to the copyrighted material itself, the copyright holder has the right to publish, display and adapt the work from one form to another and may transmit it by telecommunication. The holder may also have integrity rights; for example, an architect or artist may have the right to review any proposal to change a building or the method of displaying the work. In an alleged copyright infringement case, the legal test is whether the works can be proved to be substantially similar.

Copyright protections are also in place worldwide and are governed by the *Berne Convention*. Although some copyright practices vary from country to country, the general concepts remain the same. A copyright legal specialist can answer questions arising from international copyright issues.

The general rule of copyright is that the author is the owner, although a few notable exceptions include:

- photographs — the owner of the negative owns the copyright;
- commissioned works — the person commissioning the work is the owner;
- employment — the employer owns the work of the employee;
- in the case of an independent contractor, the contractor owns the work unless there is an agreement to the contrary.

---

[16] The *Berne Convention for the Protection of Literary and Artistic Works* was inaugurated at Paris in 1896, was revised several times to its present form (adopted also at Paris in 1971) and has been signed by 96 countries.

Enforcement of Copyright

Copyright may be enforced under either civil law or criminal law. Civil enforcement may include a court order, an injunction, the seizure of "plates" or an order for "delivery up". As well, there are several provisions in the *Criminal Code* concerning forgery and other offences relating to trade-marks or trade descriptions.[17]

Patents

Patents protect the way an idea is embodied in a product or process. In order to be patentable the idea must be useful, new and not obvious to a person skilled in the art. Patents are valid for 20 years from the date of application.

Trade Secrets

Trade secrets allow for the protection of data. To be protected, the trade secrets require relationships that include an obligation of confidentiality (*e.g.*, the employment relationship or a contract) and a secret application, formula, etc., that would affect a company financially should the data be compromised.

CONCLUSION

Because civil law is concerned with obligations between individuals and corporations, governments and others, and issues of compliance arising from those obligations, security professionals can benefit from an understanding of the basics of such relationships. As we have seen, in addition to enforcing obligations, such as contracts, security is involved in the protection of assets, the minimization of liability and risk, the prevention of negligence and in the observance of due diligence. The importance of documenting policies and procedures and providing adequate reporting has also been stressed in this chapter. The protection of intellectual property was examined and, finally, the litigation process was described, as were the judicial approaches taken to the awarding of damages.

---

[17] Sections 406 to 414.

7
Security And Human Resource Law

INTRODUCTION

In Chapter 2, "Human Rights", and Chapter 3, "The Canadian Charter of Rights and Freedoms", we noted that discriminatory practices must be avoided and that individual rights are protected under the law. This chapter describes how effective human resource policies and practices allow security professionals to conduct their operations within corporations while ensuring that human rights, Charter rights and privacy rights are protected.

Security has an important role to play in the effective management of human resources within an organization. Areas of concern include:

- internal investigations within a corporation and associated disciplinary action;
- security during strikes and labour disruptions; and
- security policies that affect the conduct of the employee population.

We begin by distinguishing between the principal aspects of human resources — employee relations and industrial or labour relations. The former deals with the common law employment relationship, while the latter deals with the trade union environment. Each of these areas is summarized in the following table:

	Employee Relations	Labour Relations
Employees	Common law employment arrangements, no collective agreement	Unionized employees
Jurisprudence	Employment Standards Acts, common law	Labour Relations Acts

Within this general framework, this chapter discusses:

- the relationship between the common law and employment practices;
- the legal aspects of operating within unionized work environments;
- how unfair labour practices may be identified and avoided;
- employment at will including termination with notice or for cause;
- how disciplinary action may be taken;
- how prosecution policies are developed; and
- ways and means of conducting internal investigations.

To summarize, this chapter provides guidelines for conducting security work under Canadian law. Practical issues will be discussed and case law examples provided to illustrate recommended policies and procedures.

EMPLOYMENT AND THE COMMON LAW

Ideally, the employee-employer relationship should be built upon a foundation of trust and openness. Dishonesty, however, is a fact of business as well as personal life and is generally considered one of the most important breaches of the employment relationship. Both the civil courts when considering a common law employment relationship and arbitrators when considering a contract relationship tend to uphold severe discipline.

In one award the arbitrator stated:[1]

> Moreover, in a very general sense, honesty is the touchstone to viable employer-employee relationships. If employees must be constantly watched to insure that they honestly report their comings and goings, or to insure that valuable tools, material and equipment are not stolen, the industrial enterprise will soon be operated on the model of a penal institution. In

---

[1] *Phillips Cables Ltd. and International Union of Electrical, Radio & Machine Workers, Local 510 (Re)* (1974), 6 L.A.C. (2d) 35 at pp. 37-8 (Ont. Arb. Bd.), affd [1978] O.J. No. 54 (QL) (Div. Ct.).

other words, employee good faith and honesty is one important ingredient to both industrial democracy and the fostering of a more co-operative labour relations climate.

The board feels that these are the sentiments underlying the arbitral castigation of dishonest conduct. Arbitrators are not equating the role of a plant to that of a church. Rather, they are insuring that the role of a plant will not evolve into a role resembling that of a penal institution.

Many arbitration awards in the contract environment have overruled an employer's decision to terminate for dishonesty and substituted a lengthy suspension, whereas the courts in the common law employment relationship have tended to hold that dishonesty merits discharge in wrongful dismissal cases.

> *The assistant treasurer of a company forged the treasurer's signature on some documents because he did not want to bother his superior while on holidays. It was urgent that the documents be signed and the assistant treasurer acted only to expedite the situation for company purposes, gaining nothing by the forgery. He was terminated and sued for wrongful dismissal. The British Columbia Supreme Court upheld the dismissal on the basis of the dishonesty in spite of the extenuating circumstances.*[2]

Much of human resource activity is directed towards fostering a trusting and respectful relationship between management and workers. Business ethics may be implied or spelled out in human resource policy statements and company standards. Policies and specific training programs set out expectations and responsibilities and define the consequences of failing to meet established employee standards. While it goes without saying that courtesy, mutual respect, co-operation and consideration foster a positive work environment and are laudable values, it is also clear that companies are particularly aware that the personal conduct of their staff members reflects back on them. A lack of honesty and trustworthiness in staff can greatly impair the public image of any business.

It is not surprising therefore that, through their human resources departments, corporations put considerable effort into developing policies that describe expectations in terms of established rules and procedures, codes of conduct, the evaluation and compensation of performance, progressive disciplinary action, appeal rights, respectful workplace policies and methods when mediating disputes. They develop health and safety programs as well as substance abuse and harassment policies, for example, to deal with potential non-compliance. Many companies offer training in these areas to

---

[2]   *Jewitt v. Prism Resources Ltd.* (1981), 127 D.L.R. (3d) 190, 30 B.C.L.R. 43 (C.A).

provide employees with basic information about their workplace rights and obligations under the law.

Where security officers are involved in internal or other investigations of allegations against an employee, they are often consulted on the appropriate discipline for the employment offence. The security department may also be the best source for advice regarding other incidents that occur in the workplace and for ensuring there is some degree of consistency in the handling of security-related disciplinary matters.

LEGAL FRAMEWORK AND UNIONIZED WORK ENVIRONMENTS

At the time of Canada's birth as a nation the trade union movement was not in any way contemplated by the founding fathers. Both federal and provincial jurisdictions, therefore, laid claim to aspects of business/labour relations. The federal Labour Code[3] applies to areas of federal jurisdiction established under the *British North America Act, 1867:*[4]

* regulation of trade
* unemployment insurance
* postal service
* navigation and shipping
* banking
* criminal law.

Provincial jurisdiction lies within the heading "property and civil rights". In spite of the broad range of federal powers, the vast majority of unionized employees are governed by provincial legislation.

The *Wagner Act* passed in the United States in 1935 has had a strong influence on Canadian labour laws. The thrust of the *Wagner Act* was the achievement of good industrial relations by:[5]

> ... encouraging the practice and procedure of collective bargaining and by protecting the exercise by workers of full freedom of association, self-organization, and designation of representatives of their own choosing, for the purpose of negotiating the terms and conditions of their employment or other mutual aid or protection.

The requirement for compulsory collective bargaining was passed in the United States during the Second World War. In Canada, compulsory col-

---

[3]   Currently the *Canada Labour Code*, R.S.C. 1985, c. L-2.
[4]   In 1982 it was renamed the *Constitution Act, 1867.*
[5]   29 U.S.C. 151. The *National Labor Relations Act*, initiated in 1935, is contained in the *United States Code*, under Title 29. The quote is part of section 151.

lective bargaining was combined with the requirement for compulsory dispute settlement.[6] Federal and provincial statutes all have:

Common Provisions	Provisions that Vary
• regulations on unfair labour practices • compulsory collective bargaining • procedures for certification and decertification of a bargaining unit	• percentage of the work population required for certification • powers of the various labour relations boards • procedures for decertification • regulations defining the bargaining unit

Section 425 of the *Criminal Code* defines prohibited conduct in terms of criminal sanctions:

> 425. Every one who, being an employer or the agent of an employer, wrongfully and without lawful authority
>
> (*a*) refuses to employ or dismisses from his employment any person for the reason only that the person is a member of a lawful trade union or of a lawful association or combination of workmen or employees formed for the purpose of advancing, in a lawful manner, their interests and organized for their protection in the regulation of wages and conditions of work,
>
> (*b*) seeks by intimidation, threat, or loss of position or employment, or by causing actual loss of position or employment, or by threatening or imposing any pecuniary penalty, to compel workmen or employees to abstain from belonging to a trade union, association or combination to which they have a lawful right to belong, or
>
> (*c*) conspires, combines, agrees or arranges with any other employer or his agent to do anything mentioned in paragraph (*a*) or (*b*),
>
> is guilty of an offence punishable on summary conviction.

Both the federal and the provincial labour statutes impose sanctions against unfair labour practices. There are four stages in the collective bargaining process:

- the organization stage — adoption or organization of a union;
- the recognition stage — certification of the union;
- the negotiation stage — bargaining process for a contract following certification;
- the administration stage — administration of the contract between employer and union.

---

6   Saskatchewan is the only province that does not address compulsory dispute settlement and, therefore, its legislation most closely parallels the United States *Wagner Act*.

A description of unfair labour practices that are associated with each of these stages follows.

The Organization Stage

Federal and provincial statutes contain similar provisions to section 425 of the *Criminal Code* regarding the refusal to hire or the firing of an employee because of union activity. In addition, they impose sanctions against providing inducements or benefits to employees in order to interfere with their right to organize. The legislation also attempts to inhibit "sweetheart arrangements" (see discussion under next heading) by prohibiting the employer from providing financial support, participating in or interfering with the formation of a trade union or with the employees' selection of the trade union that would best serve their interests.

Union representatives can be forbidden access to the employer's property (unlike in the United States) except with the employer's express permission. In exceptional circumstances, such as where the employees reside on company property (*e.g.*, in logging and mining camps), a few provinces do permit access; otherwise, union representatives are not permitted to enter. Security can, except in those special cases, legitimately refuse union organizers admittance to company property.

The Recognition Stage

The *Criminal Code* and federal and provincial labour statutes prohibit retaliation against employees who are actively involved in certification procedures. Nor may the employer modify the conditions of employment, such as wages, during the recognition stage.

Another unfair labour practice prohibited at this stage is the ratification of a "sweetheart agreement", *i.e.*, the attempt to establish a trade union that is the choice of management and not the choice of the workers. Manitoba, Ontario and Newfoundland and Labrador provide direct sanctions against this practice, while the remaining jurisdictions address it indirectly.

The Negotiation Stage

At the negotiation stage, the failure by the parties to bargain in good faith towards the goal of creating a collective agreement is recognized to be an unfair labour practice. Some provinces prohibit the employer from threatening to move or shut down operations; other jurisdictions prohibit the practice under the general sanctions against coercion.

The Administration Stage

The employer must deal fairly with all employees and must not treat a "union activist" more harshly, especially where disciplinary action is required. In such circumstances, the employee will have recourse through arbitration. The employer must also take care to avoid practices aimed at dominating, decertifying or favouring an existing union over its employees' preference.

AVOIDING UNFAIR LABOUR PRACTICES

The security department must constantly be vigilant that it does not appear to be involved in or to condone unfair labour practices. Unless handled properly, strike security, surveillance and undercover operations have the potential to infringe upon individual rights.

Undercover Operations

The use of an undercover operative is a valid investigative tool, provided it occurs under the right circumstances and with the correct degree of control. At any stage of the relationship between an employer and a trade union, the disclosure of the existence of an undercover operation may be construed as an attempt to undermine the union or gain inside information. If an operative is used, the following procedures may help to reduce the risk of being accused of improper investigative practices:

*   The undercover operative should be experienced and should be under contract with an investigative agency in order to create an arm's-length arrangement. The company should avoid using existing employees for an undercover operation because there is a stronger likelihood there will be claims of bias or of an attempt to report on union activity.
*   The contract with the investigative firm should clearly specify the scope of the assignment. It should stipulate that the operative is not being hired to report on union activity and, furthermore, should withhold any information on that topic.
*   Reports prepared by the operative should be reviewed by the contract agency before they are forwarded to the company to ensure that they do not contain information that could be construed as union activity intelligence gathering.

> *In an unreported labour relations case a security firm was hired to place undercover operatives in the picket lines to incite the picketers to violence. The company could then videotape the violence and use the video to get an injunction against the union. The union found out*

about the undercover operatives and heavy fines were issued against the employer and the security firm.

Strikes

Uniformed security officers must be trained to react and respond appropriately when strikes occur. It is imperative that the guard force receives training that clearly defines its role: its only function during a strike at a facility is to protect company assets. Security personnel should not become involved in arguments at the picket line nor attempt to put across the company's views and should not interfere with the activities of the picketers unless company property and/or personnel are jeopardized by the picketers' actions.

Interviews

A member of a trade union or association who is to be interviewed as a witness or a suspect during a security investigation should be given the opportunity to have union representation present.

General

Security rules, policies and procedures should be universal in nature and consistently applied to union and non-union personnel alike. In a unionized environment, security officers should receive their training from staff possessing expertise in labour relations matters. A security program will lose its effectiveness if the security department develops a reputation for only acting on behalf of the interests of management.

EMPLOYMENT AT WILL

Employment is a contract although, in the non-union (common law) environment, it is often implied, *i.e.*, there may be no actual signed document. In the unionized environment a collective agreement constitutes the contract between the workers and the employer and precludes the employer from terminating an employee without having "just cause". In a common law employment relationship, an employer does not need just cause to terminate an employee; however, if there is no cause the employee must be paid notice or be given an appropriate notice period.

Just cause may be a recurring employment offence where the employee has been warned, put on probation, or where there is some other form of progressive discipline. Just cause may also be one serious offence, such as an act of dishonesty. In the common law employment relationship, where just cause is not necessary for termination and the employer wishes to terminate the employee, notice of termination is all that is required or provided. Notice may consist of an appropriate sum of money equal to the period of notice or it may provide the opportunity to continue working and be paid during that period of time. If the employee sues for wrongful dismissal because the notice is insufficient, the courts will look at a number of factors, including the age of the employee, the level of responsibility, the number of years of employment and the likelihood of re-employment. The courts look at notice as a financial cushion while seeking re-employment; factors such as age and level of responsibility govern how long it will take to find another job. Labour standards legislation provides minimum requirements for notice, but in the case of higher level positions they will not generally be sufficient to meet the notice required.

> *The manager of a convenience store is suspicious that a clerk has been stealing money. There is insufficient evidence to terminate for cause so the manager terminates the employee without cause and pays the notice required by the provincial labour standards legislation. The clerk is 49 years of age and has worked at the store for 14 years. He sues for wrongful dismissal and is succesful in arguing that, in spite of the fact that he works for near minimum wage, his age and length of employment should have been taken into consideration.*

Intentional infliction of mental suffering is now also a viable cause of action for termination.[7] Thus, a company should ensure that a termination is properly handled.

> *A bank investigator conducts an inquiry concerning a loans manager whom he suspects has friends in organized crime and who may be committing fraud. The investigator convinces a police officer to lay charges. At the preliminary inquiry the matter is dismissed after the judge has heard only one witness. The former loans officer sues for wrongful dismissal and intentional infliction of mental suffering. He is able to prove in his action that he is now virtually unemployable in the banking industry as a result of the allegations. The court awards substantial damages against the bank for the notice period and for mental suffering.[8]*

---

[7] In *Wallace v. United Grain Growers Ltd.* (1997), 152 D.L.R. (4th) 1 at para. 74, [1997] 3 S.C.R. 701, the Supreme Court of Canada suggested that, where mental distress results from bad faith conduct during a summary dismissal, a trial judge has discretion to extend the period of reasonable notice. The court stated that, in the course of dismissing an employee, an employer must be "candid, reasonable, honest and forthright" with the employee and should refrain from conduct that is "unfair or is in bad faith by being, for example, untruthful, misleading or unduly insensitive" (at para. 98).

[8] See *Ribeiro v. Canadian Imperial Bank of Commerce* (1992), 13 O.R. (3d) 278, 44 C.C.E.L. 165 (C.A.), leave to appeal to S.C.C. refused 65 O.A.C. 79n, 157 N.R. 400n, for an example of a case where the punitive damages, awarded against the employer as a result of an investigation where criminal charges were laid against

The use of proper internal investigative methods and the necessity for thoroughness are critical. Mishandled investigations and heavy handedness may result in substantial awards, including punitive damages, in a wrongful dismissal action.

DISCIPLINE

There are six levels of discipline available to an employer. For recurring minor infractions by the same employee the employer may decide to start with the lower levels of discipline and gradually and progressively work up to the more severe measures until the employee changes behaviour or is terminated. Where there is one serious breach, the employer may decide to opt immediately for a severe form of discipline.

The progressive levels of discipline from the minor to major forms are:

1. *Counselling* — A discussion between the employee and the supervisor, usually at the time of the infraction.
2. *Oral warning* — A caution by the supervisor for a slightly more serious breach or a continued infraction where counselling was ineffective.
3. *Written warning* — A letter placed on the employee's personnel file as a record of the infraction and the warning given.
4. *Suspension* — Suspensions may be either:
   - *Disciplinary*: This is usually the last form of discipline before termination. Disciplinary suspensions may be either: (i) without pay; or (ii) with pay. Suspension with pay is not common but may be given to allow the employee time to reflect, obtain counselling, etc.
   - *Non-disciplinary*: These suspensions occur most often where the employee is the subject of an ongoing investigation and cannot be allowed on the worksite.
5. *Demotion* — Demotions may be either:
   - *Disciplinary*: This happens usually for a fixed period of time as a result of a particular infraction.
   - *Non-disciplinary*: This is usually the result of a performance issue, such as a physical or emotional impairment, and usually for an unspecified period.
6. *Termination* — The discharge of the employee for cause.

---

an employee even though there was little supportive evidence, were substantially increased (from $10,000 to $20,000 for mental distress, and from $10,000 to $50,000 for punitive damages).

In assessing the appropriate discipline for an employment offence, the employer should consider a number of issues, including:

- *Age* — The older employee is less likely to be able to re-enter the job market if terminated.
- *Seniority* — The long-term employee should be treated with greater leniency, especially where the person has given otherwise good service.
- *Marital status* — The spouse or children of the employee are often the victims of the employee's act and the subsequent discipline. The employer should consider the effect on them.
- *Dollar amount involved* — The economic or other effects on the employer should be considered and whether they resulted from carelessness, theft, sabotage, vandalism or a serious safety infraction.
- *Premeditation* — An act done with planning and deliberation should be dealt with more seriously than one performed on the spur of the moment.
- *Previous record* — In considering the previous employment record of the accused, the employer should only have regard for the actual documented issues on the employee's file. Rumour, the opinion of supervisors given verbally and general impressions cannot be used to support any decision concerning appropriate discipline if the case goes to arbitration or a civil hearing.
- *Degree of co-operation* — Where an employee shows remorse and co-operates in the investigation or recovery of loss there should be greater leniency than in a case where the employee denies the offence and is uncooperative.
- *Whether the company policy was published* — An employee may raise the defence that there was no published company policy indicating that certain behaviour was prohibited, or that there was no indication of what discipline would be enforced for the discredited behaviour. Employers should, for example, openly communicate company policies in relation to acts of dishonesty and should indicate that the appropriate discipline is termination of the employee in question. The policy should be universally applied on a consistent basis and should be republished each time a significant incident occurs.

PROSECUTION POLICIES

Employees Under Police Investigation

The employer's response to a police investigation involving an employee will vary according to the nature of the investigation. Let us suppose a situation where a female employee alleges that she was sexually assaulted at the worksite by a male employee. There are two possible scenarios:

- *Scenario one* — The female employee goes directly to the police and reports the matter for their investigation.
- *Scenario two* — The female employee calls security and they attend, call the police and assist the police with their investigation.

In scenario one, the company is not privy to the facts or the available evidence and may not know all of the facts unless or until the male employee is charged and there is a trial. Unless security conducts a parallel investigation, the only recourse for the company is suspension of the male employee pending trial. Once the facts are made known (either by the prosecutor following a "guilty" plea, or by evidence submitted at trial if the plea was "not guilty"), they may be used by the company to reach a decision on discipline. In scenario two, where security assists the police, the company is privy to the facts and can make a decision on discipline as soon as the investigation is finished.

Prosecution Concerns of Employers

Many corporations will discharge for dishonesty but are reluctant to prosecute, either because they fear that a police investigation will cause embarrassment to the company and bring it into disrepute or because of some misconceptions about the consequences of criminal charges. Be aware of the following:

1. *A criminal charge is not double jeopardy* — Double jeopardy only exists where the Crown Prosecutor elects to proceed against an accused who has already been convicted (*autrefois convict*) or has been acquitted (*autrefois acquit*) of the *same* charge. The decision to lay criminal charges by the police or prosecutor has no effect on the right of the employer to consider appropriate discipline.
2. *Appropriate discipline will not be affected by what occurs in criminal court* — The only evidence that will be admissible before an arbitrator or judge in a wrongful dismissal action is a guilty plea by the employee to a criminal charge related to the incident. The judge or arbitrator should not consider evidence that an accused has been acquitted or that he or she pleaded "not guilty" and was convicted. The reasons why the results of the criminal proceeding are not considered when determining the appropriate company discipline response are:
    - The issues are generally different. In a criminal trial, the Crown must prove that the accused committed a specific offence within the *Criminal Code*. In deciding on appropriate discipline, the

employer considers the much broader issue of whether the employment relationship was breached.

- There is a different burden of proof even if the issues are identical (see the discussion in Chapter 8, "Evidence").
- In criminal court, the employee may have been acquitted on a technicality that does not affect the issue at arbitration or in a civil trial. There may have been a defect in the wording of the charge or a witness may not have been available for the trial.

3. *Proceedings in one jurisdiction will not jeopardize what is happening in another* — Many companies are under the false impression that if a police investigation is underway, they must wait until it is finished before making a decision on appropriate discipline. In fact, they may decide to wait if there are good, practical reasons for doing so (evidence that may come out at trial, etc.), but they may also make their own decision irrespective of the police investigation. It is not unusual for simultaneous actions to be underway in criminal court, civil court and/or before an arbitration panel for the situation under scrutiny.

4. *Criminal charges are not a form of discipline* — When a prosecutor or the police decide to lay charges they are not acting on behalf of the employer. A decision by an employer to turn the matter over to the police and "let them handle it" is a decision to not undertake any form of discipline.

A prosecution policy gets the message out to employees that "we are good corporate citizens and obey the law and we expect our employees and others to do the same". Failure to prosecute may lead employees to think the company is unwilling to go to the police because it has something to hide. The general public wisdom is that the only people afraid to go to the police are criminals.

CONDUCTING INTERNAL INVESTIGATIONS

The conduct of an internal investigation is one of a security department's most important tasks. The security investigator must ensure that the rights of the employee to confidentiality, the rights of the corporation to a thorough assessment of the facts and the proper protection of evidence are duly maintained. The Model for Internal Investigation chart (see next page) describes the systematic approach used by security investigators when conducting inquiries within unionized and non-unionized environments alike.

Model for Internal Investigation

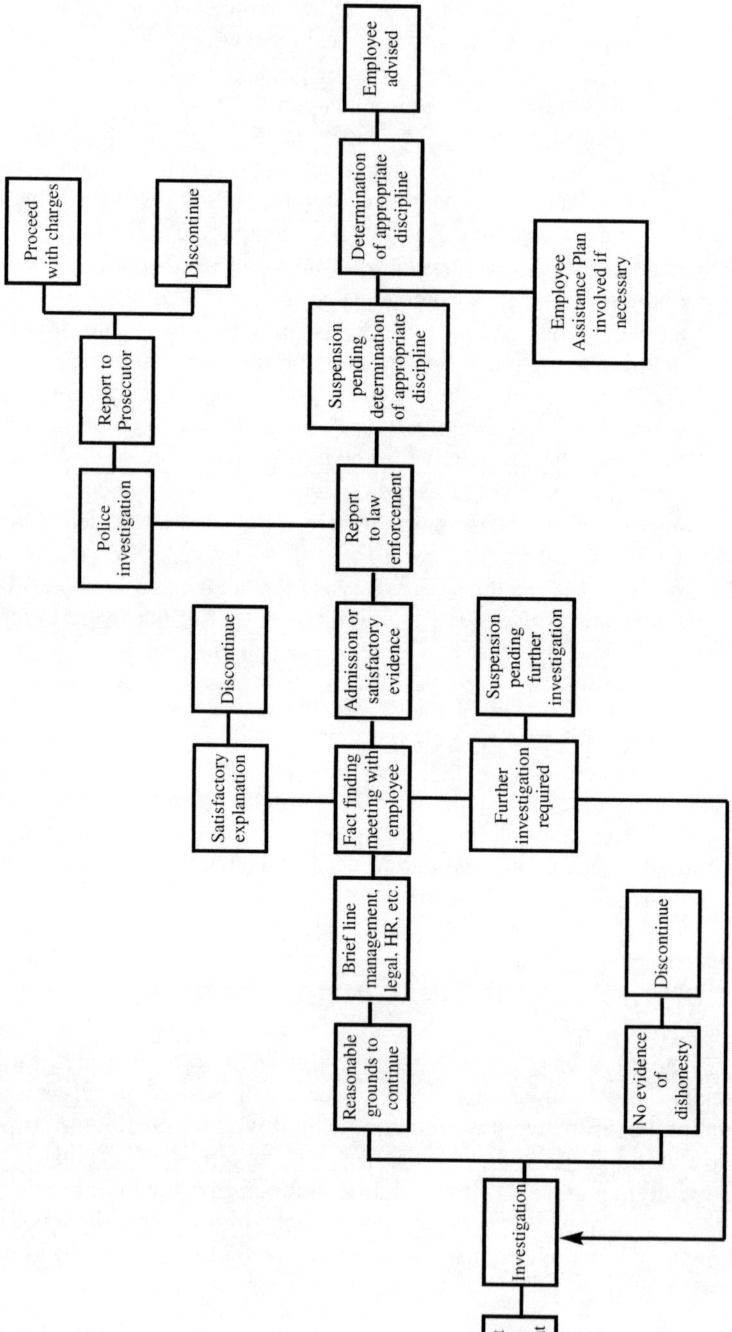

Fact-finding Meetings

A fact-finding meeting is more than the interview of an employee suspected of a criminal or employment offence. If management has misgivings about an employee and is considering discipline, they have a duty to present their suspicions to that employee so that a response and/or explanation for the questionable behaviour can be given. The fact-finding meeting has several benefits for management:

1. If an employee sues or the employee's complaint goes to arbitration, management is in a much better position to show that their decision was made after gathering all of the facts and was not made "in the heat of anger".
2. It allows management to put questions to the employee before there is a chance to create an alibi.
3. If the employee lies during a fact-finding meeting, the employer will have a stronger case. Lying in response to questions put during a fact-finding meeting is a punishable offence in itself and it is also sound evidence of guilt.
4. Information received during the fact-finding meeting can be used to develop further evidence.

Fact-finding meetings are different from police interviews in that the Charter protections need not be applied in those circumstances.[9] In the employment relationship there is no procedural fairness requirement, nor any right to be informed of the right to counsel and the right against self-incrimination. The corporation will, in its dealings with employees under suspicion, treat them according to its own proper business ethics and code of conduct. Neither strong-arming an employee into making a confession nor resorting to violent accusatory outbursts is appropriate under any circumstances in the conduct of business affairs. It also goes without saying that, as an implied condition of employment, there is a duty on the part of an employee to co-operate with the employer. Failure to co-operate may constitute the disciplinary offence of insubordination. Depending on the severity of the insubordination and the strength of the employer's case, various sanctions may be applied up to and including termination.[10] An employee may still have recourse at common law to torts such as unlawful confinement, assault and battery, if the interview technique is deemed inappropriate.

---

[9] See *Reed v. Canada* (1989), 41 C.R.R. 371, [1989] C.T.C. 192 (F.C.T.D.), affd 2 C.R.R. (2d) 192 (C.A.); *R. v. Shafie* (1989), 47 C.C.C. (3d) 27, 68 C.R. (3d) 259 (C.A.).

[10] See *Robert Hunt Corp. and CJA, Local 3054 (Re)* (1982), 4 L.A.C. (3d) 14 (Ont. Arb. Bd.); *George Lanthier et Fils Ltee and Milk and Bread Drivers, Caterers and Allied Employees, Local 647 (Re)* (1987), 31 L.A.C. (3d) 320 (Ont. Arb. Bd.).

During a criminal investigation, the security officer must decide whether or not to Charter caution an employee.[11] A Charter caution removes the duty on the part of the employee to co-operate with the employer's investigation; however, at the same time, once cautioned, any admission by the employee to the accusations may be entered into evidence at a future criminal trial.

At the end of the fact-finding meeting, unless the issue is very straightforward and does not require any further inquiry, management should take some time to determine appropriate discipline. If the issue is a particularly serious one, management may even consider suspension of the employee with or without pay for a short period to afford company leaders the time necessary to decide whether discipline is appropriate and what it should be. Such a delay also sends the message that the decision to enforce sanctions against the employee was not made in the heat of anger. This reaction is especially valuable in cases where the accused employee later brings forward a wrongful dismissal action. Without question, this is a difficult period for the employee involved. Management should, as a matter of course, offer the employee the services of a psychological counsellor.

CONCLUSION

The focus of this chapter has been to provide the legal context for security work within unionized and non-unionized work environments. Employment in a common law context and under Labour Relations Acts were compared and their relationship to the security industry was shown. Appropriate behaviour for security professionals conducting undercover work, during strike conditions and during investigations was also emphasized.

---

[11]   See Chapter 8, "Evidence", for a detailed discussion of the term "Charter caution".

8

Evidence

INTRODUCTION

When a case is brought to trial, it must be proved or disproved on the basis of the evidence presented. Evidence may include (but is not limited to) witness testimony, documentation, and surveillance information, as well as any biological and forensic materials collected by the crime scene investigators. In a criminal trial, the collected evidence is catalogued as a series of exhibits any of which the trial judge may allow or disallow. The manner in which evidence is introduced and presented is governed by the "rules of evidence" that must be observed by all parties participating in the trial. In fact, the "law of evidence determines how facts may be proved in a court of law and what facts may not be proved there".[1] Objections and questions raised by counsel concerning the improper introduction of evidence are a common occurrence at trial. After all, a lawyer must act in the best interests of his or her client. During the questioning of a witness, for example, a question deemed improper under the rules of evidence may well result in testimony being excluded or being stricken from the record, which means it must be disregarded by the judge or jury hearing the case. As this example illustrates, the introduction of evidence at trial is subject to the application of a complex code.

GATHERING AND INTRODUCING EVIDENCE AT TRIAL

Examination-in-Chief

Based on his or her knowledge of the events at issue, the party calling the witness (*e.g.*, the prosecutor calling a police officer, or defence coun-

---

[1] R. Cross and N. Wilkins, *An Outline of the Law of Evidence*, 3rd ed. (London: Butterworths, 1971).

sel calling the defendant) introduces the witness's qualifications to testify during the examination-in-chief. Leading questions may not be asked (*i.e.*, those in which the mere phrasing of the questions suggests the answers desired), although there are a few exceptions to this rule:

- To establish information that is undisputed, leading questions may be used to speed up the examination process. For example, questions such as "Your name is John Doe? Are you a security officer with XYZ Company?" are expected to be answered in the affirmative and serve only to quickly establish the known identity of the witness.
- In criminal cases, in certain very restricted circumstances, the prosecutor may introduce a prior inconsistent statement by a witness.
- Where the judge has granted leave to treat a witness as hostile, direct questions may be asked during the examination-in-chief.

Cross-examination

In cross-examination, however, the party who did not call the witness is allowed to ask direct and leading questions.

COMPETENCE AND COMPELLABILITY

Competence refers to whether a witness has the legal capability to testify. Once competence has been determined, compellability refers to whether the witness can be legally forced to testify.

What Affects Competence?

Mental incapacity and extreme youth are obvious issues that can affect the competence of a witness to testify at trial. In such cases, the judge may put questions to the witness to find out if he or she fully appreciates the duty to speak the truth under oath.

What Affects Compellability?

Several factors can interfere with the ability to compel a witness to testify:

- *Diplomatic immunity* — Those entitled to diplomatic immunity may be competent but are not compellable as witnesses.
- *Accused* — Under the *Canadian Charter of Rights and Freedoms* an accused person cannot be obliged by the prosecution to take the stand to give evidence, thereby running the risk of incriminating himself or herself. If the accused does choose to give evidence, however, he or she may then be cross-examined by the prosecutor.

- *Spouse of the accused* — The spouse of an accused person cannot be compelled to give evidence regarding communications between the partners during the marriage.
- *Privilege* — In certain cases, communications between solicitor and client are not admissible in court against the client. Any discussion between a lawyer and client with a view to obtaining legal advice or in contemplation of litigation would not be admissible, but discussions relating to business advice or evidence of communications relating to a conspiracy to which the lawyer is a party may be admissible in court. The law does not recognize any other form of privileged communication (*e.g.*, accountants, psychiatrists, doctors or clergy).

TYPES OF EVIDENCE

Direct and Circumstantial Evidence

Evidence is "direct" when a witness can testify that knowledge of it came by way of one or more of the five senses (*i.e.*, taste, smell, sight, touch and hearing). An example of direct evidence would be testimony from a witness who observed the accused draw a gun and pull the trigger and who then heard a shot ring out and saw the victim fall to the ground. Circumstantial evidence, on the other hand, is derived from inference. Testimony by the witness that he or she saw the accused standing over the body of the victim with a smoking gun is, therefore, circumstantial. Contrary to popular belief, circumstantial evidence is admissible and, in fact, most of the evidence entered at trial is circumstantial. It is the responsibility of the witness to relate the events or facts as the witness knows them; it is then up to the judge or jury to decide whether the circumstantial evidence leads to an inference of a fact that would convict the accused.

Primary and Secondary Evidence

Evidence is also grouped into primary and secondary classifications. Primary evidence suggests that it is the "best evidence" available whereas secondary evidence suggests that there is something better. For example, a copy of a document is secondary evidence; the original is primary evidence. The "best evidence" rule requires the production of the truest or most authentic evidence available. However, in some cases there is a statutory override. The *Canada Evidence Act*[2] allows the admission of banking and business documents as proof of their contents even though the Crown may have available the *viva voce* (in person) testimony of a witness.

---

[2]   R.S.C. 1985, c. C-5, sections 29 and 30.

Hearsay and Exceptions to Hearsay

The general rule against hearsay evidence is that assertions other than those of the witness who is testifying are inadmissible as evidence of the truth of the thing asserted. An example is an attempt by a witness to repeat what another person said. The practical reason for the rule is that the court should hear the testimony directly from the person who uttered the words, rather than repeated by someone else. Most rules in law are more important for their exceptions and the rule on hearsay is no different. A few of the more important exceptions follow:

1. *Opinion or expert evidence* — In most cases, opinion is not acceptable as evidence. However, where one of the parties is able to establish that a witness is competent to form an opinion on some subject because of a special course of study or experience, counsel may be allowed to enter that opinion evidence into the court record.

2. *Business and banking documents* — Business and banking documents are admitted into evidence as truth of their contents in spite of the fact that no person is providing *viva voce* testimony as to their accuracy. In a complex commercial crime prosecution it is possible for the Crown to submit its entire case by means of introducing business and banking documents without recourse to any human witnesses.

3. *Dying declarations* — Hearsay evidence of a statement relating to the cause of death made by the person who is dying is admissible in court. The Crown must prove that the person making the original statement was under expectation of death and would otherwise have been a competent witness.

4. *Res gestae* — Statements made *res gestae* (spontaneously) that are simultaneous with and directly related to the facts at issue are another example of hearsay evidence that may be admissible from another witness. In *R. v. Fowkes*,[3] a police officer was in the room with a father and son when a shot came through the window. The son apparently saw a face at the window and shouted out the nickname of the person he saw before being struck and killed. The police officer did not see the face at the window but was allowed to testify with respect to the son's statement at trial identifying the person who fired the fatal shot.

---

[3]   *Times* (March 8, 1856). The case was referred to by Sir J.F. Stephen (1829-94) in article 8 of his discussion of *res gestae*: see *A Digest of the Law of Evidence*, 12th ed. (rev.), by H.L. Stephen and L.F. Sturge (London: Macmillan, 1946).

5. *Affidavits and depositions* — Under some statutes, affidavits and dep-
    ositions (written statements made under oath) are admissible in court
    as truth of their content.[4]

6. *Admissions and confessions* — A confession is a written or oral state-
    ment, not made in court, against the interest of the accused. Such
    statements may be inculpatory (those that are incriminating to the
    accused) or exculpatory (a denial by the accused that turns out to be a
    lie and is therefore considered evidence of guilt). For example, a
    statement by the accused such as "I did it and I'm sorry" is inculpa-
    tory. A statement by the accused that "I didn't do it because I was
    somewhere else at the time" (where that statement is later proven
    false) is exculpatory.

Admissibility of Confessions

Three issues are involved in determining the admissibility of confessions into evidence:

- relevance;
- voluntariness; and
- whether the confession is made to a person in authority.

It Must Be Relevant

A statement will obviously not be admissible in court if it is irrelevant
to the issue being tried. A relevant statement will reflect on the guilt of the
accused by being either:

- a direct admission of the act or one of the required elements of the
  act (inculpatory); or
- an alibi or other self-serving statement that can be disproved by
  other evidence (exculpatory).

> *An employee is under investigation for theft of tools from a shop. When
> interviewed initially, he states that he did not take the tools. Under a
> search warrant, the tools are later recovered from his residence and he
> makes the statement to police that he had authority from the shop fore-
> man to remove the tools. Both statements are relevant and admissible
> to the guilt of the accused, even though they are both self-serving and
> contradict each other.*

A professional investigator will take detailed notes of any statements
made by a suspect because often the relevance of a statement may not
become obvious until later in the investigation.

---

[4]   Sections 29 and 30 of the *Canada Evidence Act* allow affidavit evidence in support
      of books and records.

It Must Be Voluntary

There has been a great deal of discussion in case law about the need for a statement to be voluntary. The concern of the courts is that if a statement is given by an accused under a threat or a promise it is less likely to be reliable. This leads to the question: "Did the accused make the confession because it is true or did he or she offer the confession as a result of the threat or promise of the interrogator?"

A threat does not necessarily have to be a threat of violence against the accused. In a security investigation of an employee, a threat to terminate the employment of the suspect may be sufficient reason to exclude a statement. A promise need not be something as obvious as "Tell me what happened and I will let you go". A promise with words such as "Things will go better for you if you tell me what happened" may be sufficient to render a statement inadmissible.

The procedure adopted by the courts is that once the Crown Prosecutor stipulates that a confession will be put forward the trial enters into a *voir dire* stage (a trial within a trial). During the *voir dire*, the trial of the issue stops and the Crown begins entering evidence to establish that the statement was voluntary. The accused will have the opportunity to enter evidence that the statement was not given voluntarily and the judge will then make a decision as to whether the statement should be admitted in evidence. If it is a jury trial, the jury will be excluded during the *voir dire*. When they return either the statement evidence will be presented, if the judge has decided to allow it, or the Crown will be expected to proceed with other evidence, if it has been disallowed. The judge decides whether the statement is free and voluntary and the jury decides whether it is true.

It Must Be Made to a Person in Authority

A *voir dire* is necessary where a confession is made to a person in authority thereby creating a higher burden on the authority to establish the voluntary nature of the confession. A "person in authority" includes not only the police but also "those whom the prisoner might reasonably suppose to be capable of influencing the course of prosecution". An employer is a person in authority, especially where the offence is against the employer, and under most circumstances that includes security officers since they are assigned by the employer or property owner to protect the assets of the organization. Where a confession is made to someone who is not a person in authority, it is not necessary to hold a *voir dire* to establish the voluntary nature of the statement.

The following are examples of relationships that have been identified by the courts as "persons in authority":

- the father of a rape victim when questioning his daughter's attacker;

- an Indian agent dealing with natives on a reserve;
- masters with their servants;
- the captain of a vessel;
- the Crown Prosecutor;
- the parent of an accused where they are actively involved in questioning.

But not:

- a physician with a patient;
- police informers;
- a bank employee in connection with a former employee.

The Judges' Rules were established in England as guidelines for the police and included a caution to be given to an accused prior to a statement being taken. For many years in Canada the police followed the Judges' Rules caution, even though it was not required at that time by legislation. With the enactment in 1982 of the *Canadian Charter of Rights and Freedoms*, the person in authority taking the statement was required to advise the accused person of the right to counsel in order to ensure that the statement would be admissible in evidence.

The Decision to Caution the Accused

In the course of a security investigation where an accused is being questioned after an arrest, the security officer is performing a "governmental function" and should give the suspect a Charter caution. Where the statement is being taken in the course of a non-governmental function — for example, an internal company security investigation — the Charter caution may not apply. The security officer must elect whether to caution the accused, based on the following questions:

1. Is the primary reason for the investigation a decision on internal company discipline or is it to provide the police with evidence to prosecute as a criminal matter?
2. Will the reading of the Charter caution reduce the likelihood that the suspect will be willing to give a statement?

Where the arrested person asks to be represented by a lawyer or trade union representative during the course of an internal investigation (whether the Charter caution has been given or not), the interview should be stopped and the individual should be afforded the right to representation.

Sample of a Charter Caution

A Charter caution is issued under section 10(*b*) of the *Canadian Charter of Rights and Freedoms*. The Charter caution released by the Alberta Department of Justice reads:

> You have the right to retain and instruct counsel without delay. This means that before we proceed with our investigation you may call any lawyer you wish or get free legal advice from duty counsel immediately. If you want to call duty counsel, we will provide you with a telephone and you can call a toll-free number provided by the Legal Aid Society of Alberta for free, immediate legal advice. On weekends, and between the hours of 5:00 p.m. and 8:00 a.m. on weekdays, that number is 1-866-653-3424. Between the hours of 8:00 a.m. and 5:00 p.m. on weekdays, you may obtain free, immediate legal advice by calling any lawyer whose number may be given by the Law Society's Lawyer Referral Service at 1-800-661-1095. If you wish to contact any other lawyer, a telephone and telephone book will be provided to you. If you are charged with an offence, you may apply to Legal Aid for assistance. Do you understand? Do you want to call duty counsel or any other lawyer?

The response required to be made to an accused who waives his or her right to counsel reads:

> You have a constitutional right to a reasonable opportunity to contact a lawyer. During this time, we cannot take a statement from you or ask you to participate in any process that might provide evidence against you. You may receive free and immediate, preliminary advice at any time during our investigation by calling the toll free number provided by the Legal Aid Society. By deciding not to contact a lawyer, you should understand that you are waiving your right to receive legal advice about our investigation. Do you now wish to waive your right to receive free and immediate, preliminary legal advice or legal advice from any lawyer you wish?

Principles to be Observed in Taking a Confession

The Judges' Rules have historically provided some guidance to police when taking confessions. The following guidelines may also be helpful to security professionals:

1. The suspect must be offered a chance to contact counsel and should be given the opportunity to carry on a private conversation.
2. The object of the interview is to learn the truth, not to induce a pattern of deceit or obtain answers that the questioner wants to hear.
3. There should be no actual or implied threats or promises.
4. The accused should be given the opportunity to give a full explanation.

5. The accused should be questioned in language and phraseology that he or she understands — "legalese" or technical terms unknown to the accused should be avoided.
6. The interviewer should not ask ambiguous questions.
7. The interviewer should prepare and write down key questions prior to the interview session in order to ensure that nothing of importance is omitted.
8. The interviewer should not be aggressive or abusive to the person being interviewed.
9. An audio or video recording of the interview may prove to be helpful at the time of trial. A recording will serve to confirm what was actually said by the accused and that no threats or promises were made.

DISCOVERY

Since the *Stinchcombe* case,[5] there has been a greater onus on the Crown to provide complete disclosure to the accused. Without having to make a request, the accused is entitled to:

- receive a copy of the criminal record;
- receive a copy of any statements made by the accused to a person in authority and recorded in writing or to inspect the statement if it was recorded by electronic means;
- inspect any proposed evidence to be submitted and be provided with a copy, where practical;
- receive a copy of the "will state" (the evidence that the witnesses are expected to swear to at trial);
- receive any information known to the Crown that would be in the accused's favour;
- receive criminal records of proposed witnesses; and
- receive the name and address of any person who might have information useful to the accused.

BURDEN OF PROOF

Ultimately, the object of the trial process is to persuade the judge and jury that enough facts exist to prove the allegations of the case being prosecuted. Different levels of proof are required depending on the type of case under consideration. The burden of proof that is necessary will depend on the nature of the issue and the forum in which it is being heard.

---

[5]   *R. v. Stinchcombe* (1995), 96 C.C.C. (3d) 318, [1995] 1 S.C.R. 754.

Society demands a higher burden of proof wherever the legal repercussions are greater.

Burden of Proof at Criminal, Civil and Arbitration Hearings

Balance of Probabilities	Preponderance of Evidence	Beyond a Reasonable Doubt
Civil Labour Arbitration (other than dishonesty)	Labour Arbitration (dishonesty)	Criminal

Balance of Probabilities

The balance of probabilities is the lowest burden of proof and applies to the adjudication of civil issues between two parties and to labour arbitration cases that do not involve dishonesty (*e.g.*, a termination due to poor performance). The burden is on the plaintiff to prove the issue at a civil trial and is on the employer at arbitration.

Preponderance of Evidence

Somewhere in between the "balance of probabilities" and "beyond a reasonable doubt" is the standard of "a preponderance of evidence" which applies to the review of dishonesty cases at arbitration. The reason for the higher standard developed for dishonesty cases is best stated as follows:[6]

> The social effects upon one having been found guilty of stealing by an established arbitration tribunal may not be as far reaching as if a judicial body had made the finding; yet, the effects upon the public mind, which might be reasonably impressed by the fact that a formalized tribunal to settle industrial disputes issued judgment, would be far greater than if an employee were discharged by an employer on a charge of stealing and no impartial hearing were held.

The burden is on the employer to establish the case at arbitration on an issue of dishonesty:[7]

---

[6] *Freuhauf-Carter Division and International Union of Electrical, Radio & Machinists, Talbot Lodge 61 (Re)* (1954), 21 L.A. 832.

[7] *Toronto (Metropolitan) and CUPE, Local 79 (DaSilva) (Re)* (1992), 28 L.A.C. (4th) 160 (Ont. Arb. Bd.), at p. 169.

Arbitrators are in general agreement that the application of these principles to grievances arising out of discipline or discharge for misconduct of a criminal or *quasi*-criminal nature requires that the employer prove the misconduct by clear, strong and cogent evidence.

An arbitration panel is not bound by the formal rules of evidence and the only grounds for appeal of its decision are procedural issues.

Beyond a Reasonable Doubt

This is the highest burden that can be applied to the trial of an issue and is reserved for the Crown in proving an accused guilty at a criminal trial.

VIDEO SURVEILLANCE

The video camera has probably had a greater effect on the security industry than any other modern device. Cameras are now widely used in industry to monitor the worksite, as an investigative tool to record criminal activity and to gather evidence on malingering employees. In spite of the fact that there is strong legislation regulating the recording of private communications, there are no similar provisions restricting the use of video recording. Some unions have negotiated privacy clauses into their contracts, but aside from those particular situations, the employer is free to implement video surveillance at the worksite.[8]

The only restriction that the security officer should be aware of is the possibility that the submission of video evidence may be excluded at a criminal trial where the suspect is able to establish a breach of the right to privacy under section 8 of the Charter or under privacy legislation. This restriction also applies in criminal cases as a result of the decision in *R. v. Wong*.[9] Police are required to obtain court authorization to install video surveillance if they wish to use it as evidence in court. Security staff do not require a court authorization but should be in a position to demonstrate that there were reasonable grounds to believe that criminal or employment infractions were being committed prior to the installation of the video equipment and that all other available investigative means were pursued prior to the implementation of the surveillance. The test that the court or arbitrator will apply is the balance between the probative value of the videotaped evidence and its prejudicial effect on the privacy of employees. Videos that require enhancement will probably be inadmissible.

---

[8] For further treatment of this topic see E. Goldstein, *Visual Evidence: A Practitioner's Manual* (Toronto: Carswell, 1991) (looseleaf).

[9] (1991), 60 C.C.C. (3d) 460, [1990] 3 S.C.R. 36.

The federal Privacy Commissioner has suggested that four questions should be asked before video surveillance is undertaken:

* Is the measure demonstrably necessary to meet a specific need?
* Is it likely to be effective in meeting that need?
* Is the loss of privacy proportional to the benefit gained?
* Is there a less privacy-invasive way of achieving the same end?

A British Columbia case provides a good example of the exclusion of videotaped surveillance evidence for privacy reasons.[10] In that case, an employee went on sick leave because of the flu. The employer hired private investigators who videotaped the employee, while he was absent on "sick leave", giving instructions and working at a construction site. When the employee returned to work, he was asked what he did while off. He stated that he had simply stayed at home to recuperate from the flu. The employee was terminated and his case went to arbitration. The arbitrator, in discussing the need to balance the employee's right to privacy and the employer's right to investigate, disallowed the video evidence. He stated that there was a lack of evidence to support use of the video surveillance in the first place. In addition, he maintained that because the employer failed to first confront the employee with any suspicions about the person's alleged malingering, it had in effect set a trap. The arbitrator concluded that the employee should first have been queried about the nature of his illness, the effect it would have on his capacity to work and whether he intended to do anything else while off sick. In this case, the employee was reinstated but with only 50% of lost pay.

The courts will accept videotaped evidence where the Crown or the employer can establish that there is no expectation of privacy at the worksite.[11] A company is in a much stronger position to prove its case if it can demonstrate that its employees have been informed that their on-site activities are being continuously videotaped.

ADMISSIBILITY AND USE OF THE POLYGRAPH

The polygraph is an instrument used by law enforcement and security to record changes in cardiovascular, respiratory and electro-dermal pat-

---

[10] *Doman Forest Products Ltd. and IWA, Local 1-357 (Re)* (1990), 13 L.A.C. (4th) 275 (B.C. Arb. Bd.).

[11] *Alberta Wheat Pool and Grain Workers' Union, Local 333 (Gould) (Re)* (1995), 48 L.A.C. (4th) 332 (Alta. Arb. Bd.), provides an example of the use of video evidence to disprove an injury claim. In *R. v. LeBeau* (1988), 41 C.C.C. (3d) 163, 62 C.R. (3d) 157 (Ont. C.A.), police video surveillance of a public washroom used for acts of gross indecency was accepted into evidence because the actions of the accused indicated no expectation of privacy.

terns in an accused as he or she undergoes questioning. The results, when compared against standard results, provide a diagnostic reading about the honesty or dishonesty of the individual. The fact that an accused passed or failed a polygraph test or that he or she accepted or refused to take the test is not admissible in evidence. Should the accused provide a statement following a polygraph test, it will be admissible, subject to the usual rules for admission of statements.

The courts are also reluctant to accept polygraph results as a test of witness credibility, because the ultimate determination of credibility belongs to the trier of fact (the court).[12]

CONCLUSION

This chapter discussed how evidence is gathered, introduced and presented at trial. The types of evidence, the admissibility of evidence, its relevance to court proceedings and the notion of burden of proof were all detailed. In addition, this chapter summarized basic requirements related to arrest, confession and the use of video surveillance and polygraph evidence. By understanding the role of evidence in criminal and civil proceedings, security people can perform their functions more effectively.

Throughout this book the main thrust of the discussion and information has been directed towards providing security practitioners with comprehensive knowledge of their legal rights and obligations and an understanding of the limitations inherent in their positions. The possibility of liability as a result of a security professional's actions or inaction is a constant. To be successful, that is, to do the job well and safely, security professionals must be able to anticipate and prepare for legal challenges, must be alert to and recognize the existence of problems, and must react in a manner that not only protects their employer's best interests but also their own.

---

[12] *R. v. Beland* (1987), 43 D.L.R. (4th) 641, 36 C.C.C. (3d) 481 (S.C.C.).

Index